The XUL Reader

The XUL Reader

AN ANTHOLOGY OF ARGENTINE POETRY

1980-1996

EDITED BY ERNESTO LIVON GROSMAN

ROOF BOOKS
NEW YORK

This book was made possible, in part, by a grant from the New York State
Council on the Arts
ROOF BOOKS
are published by
The Segue Foundation
303 East 8th Street
New York, New York 10009

CONTENTS

INTRODUCTION

by Ernesto Livon Grosman

In 1994, I had the opportunity to organize a conference with poets from North and South America, including Jorge Santiago Perednik, one of the editors of the magazine XUL, David Huerta of Mexico and Charles Bernstein of the United States. James Sherry, the editor of Roof Books, was interested in the discussion presented at the conference and very generously offered to put together an anthology of some of the XUL texts published in the last sixteen years.

One of my reasons for organizing this conference revolved around the idea that a great deal of the poetry written and published by XUL during the military dictatorship constituted a means of cultural resistance. Today, in writing the introduction to this anthology, it seems important to briefly identify the different aspects of this resistance.

In the beginning of the 1980s—and in the middle of the dictatorship that started in 1976 and ended in 1983, a small poetry magazine, XUL, published its first issue. The name of the magazine alludes among other things to Xul Solar, the experimental artist and poet who had a great influence on the writings of Jorge Luis Borges.

As with other publications at the time, XUL formed part of what in retrospect I refer to as a culture of resistance. This resistance had less to do with heroics than with creative and intellectual survival. It was a resistance to the censorship of millions and the extermination of thousands of people by the military government as well as a questioning of the shortcomings of other sectors of the community as a whole. Poetry constituted a practice which—because of its independence with respect to commercial publishing houses and because of its more limited circulation in comparison with the novel and essay—received less attention on the part of the censors and permitted a revision of the criteria around which the community was organized.

In retrospect, it's tempting to think of this resistance as a confrontation between two opposites: victims and victimizers, but twenty years later it is hard to accept binary explanations at face value. For the anthologist of this collection, there is no analogy more inexact than that which assumes that there was a criminal military government on one side and a guerrilla movement on the other, assuming there was no community functioning as a nexus in fact, actively supporting one or another sector and in some cases both. The cultural environment was no exception and the challenge was to question not only the most obvious enemy but also the ideology of those who were being annihilated. It is difficult to imagine a community that did not participate, although certainly to a different degree, in the perpetuation of a strategy of extermination, something which in Argentine history was already an integral part of its institutions.

This resistance was closely associated with the discussion about the impossibility of representation, as understood by many of XUL's contributors. Representation was rejected not only because of the violence of the repression, but because many of the contributors had serious doubts about representation itself—that eagerness to fill the gap between literature and its referent. Exploring many of the social issues addressed by the novel of the 1970's, XUL also called for a discussion of poetry and writing in which politics and formal experimentation were no longer conceived as mutually exclusive. Formal experimentation made it possible for poetry to protest authoritarianism even during times of repression and censorship; as was the case in 1993 when the newly elected democratic government adopted the increasingly authoritarian attitude which so resembled its military predecessor (see "Letter to the President" in the editorial section).

Although the magazine never stopped its criticism of the dictatorship, it did not conform to the general expectation of aligning itself with the cultural agenda of the left. If the agenda of the Argentine left during the 1970's can be best defined as populist and content oriented, it is not because concerns with form were absent from it but because colloquialism—as seen in much poetry from Spanish America during that period—was believed to be the best manner in which to express those concerns because it produced an effect of transparency. XUL's refusal to adopt a didactic point of view created space within the magazine for a variety of theoretical approaches without allowing any single approach to represent the magazine as a whole. The desire to write about poetry, linguistics and Argentine culture without relying on sociological explanations made it possible to resist the strong tendency toward polarization characteristic of the times. As XUL's editor Jorge Perednik remarks in issue #4 (August 1982), "XUL's engagement with reality is found in its commitment to language: to again make legible that which has been used for coercion and deception."

This Reader is organized in such a way as to offer some of the background that was an integral part of the magazine during the first years of its publication. The genealogy presented in this selection does not represent a desire to establish an identity but to create new connections which reflect the editors' different interests. Family ties evident in this anthology are thus the result of a reorganization of the past according to the needs of the present: they are not exhaustive but offer an idea of some of the themes and issues which appeared consistently in the magazine without creating an impression of homogeneity (as if the magazine had a single editorial committee throughout its 16 year history). Other names could be part of the precursors section—writers such as Jorge Luis Borges, Juan L. Ortiz and Augusto De Campos were important points of reference among the editors of XUL. But I decided to limit this section—as well as the whole anthology—to the material published within the magazine from 1981 to 1996 offering a close up of the writing selected by the editors themselves.

At the end of the 19th century José Hernández, author of "Martín Fierro," the epic poem that narrates the history of the gauchos, explored a landscape and a style of life that has become a historical point of reference in Creole culture. Almost a century later, XUL rereads gaucho poetry because of its insistent exploration of the vernacular, but treats the vernacular as a literary device. Composed by authors who were not gauchos, turn of the century gaucho poetry appears to contain, for the contemporary reader of the 70's, a subversive element of imposture that appeals to an audience attracted to linguistics and semiotics. The gaucho poetry of the end of this century, which some of the XUL contributors referred to as "neobarroso" or "neomurkiness" cuts through censorship by invoking a canonical genre with the liberty afforded by a gesture that by now has become highly ironic. The censors overlooked parody, the magazine survived.

In many cases the poems adopted parataxis and metonymy, a strategy that brought the reader closer to the texts while challenging the new-romanticism explicitly present in other contemporary publications. Any of Jorge Lépore's poems or "Miss Murkiness" by Emeterio Cerro are a good example of how far XUL went to avoid becoming entangled in the kind of language preponderant in the literary section of the Sunday papers.

Devil Hound	turkey	chickens
ay!	the crows	of indians
ay!	history	

(tr. K.A. Kopple)

Gaucho poetry also reflects the Argentinean fascination with its own history, which in itself is a comment about the intensity of the discussion around national and personal identity—a fascination also shared by XUL. But the magazine rejected any notion of historical determinism in contrast to the cultural populists who responded to the paramilitary groups of the right with demands for legibility and transparency and whose ideological rigidity was indistinguishable from that of their persecutors. XUL does not avoid historical discourse, but, problematizes it as it is case with Néstor Perlongher's "Tuyú".

History, is it a language?
Does this language have to do with the language of history
or with the history of language?
where it stuttered/
Does it have to do with this verse?
living tongues licking dead tongues
tongues rotting like socks
tongues, lingering, fungous
this language of history/ which history?
if the long history of the tongue isn't taken as story

(tr. Molly Weigel)

Similarly, in "Patrimonies 1981" by Susana Cerdá the poem refers to the repression during the military dictatorship but history itself is put into question as yet another type of writing.

I
And after: this war
we return to be goddesses
or perhaps gods.
I ask myself with any question
mark
responding
without any
answer mark
After: (the past provoked by the verb, linked with the proposition: the only plural position that ends in preparing the place. Place of delight where one persistently searches for: EXIT. Eruption, disruption, a tear, evacuation. We have. We are being, have been thrown toward another. Place.)

(tr. Molly Weigel, Ernesto Livon Grosman)

In spite of the different poetics in XUL, this concern with history in association with formal innovation has been one of the magazine's consistent themes.

Whether it concerned recent history, as in the case of the Falkland War, or the civil war that took place during the last century, formal experimentation was understood as political resistance. Experimentation refuted the alleged separation between form and content and—because it created textual challenges which demand the reader's involvement—it provided an alternative to the didacticism of the times.

> *Jorge Luis Borges:* "Revenge does not alter what was done to you. Neither does forgiveness. Revenge and forgiveness are irrelevant."
> *Paul Theroux:* "What can you do?"
> *Jorge Luis Borges:* "Forget. That is all you can do. When something bad is done to me, I pretend that it happened a long time ago, to someone else.
>
> The Old Patagonian Express (p. 375)
> Paul Theroux

Memory and forgiveness, as Borges' answer shows, are inseparable. Together they constitute the process by which we reconstruct the past within a present that never ceases to change us, even if we pretend that it happened to someone else.

If XUL were refractory with respect to literary categories in general and to the avantgarde as a paratextual theater in particular, it is also possible to perceive an editorial interest to the Vanguards of the 1920's and 1930's and more recent manifestations of the same concerns. Xul Solar, one of the most radical but hardly the most recognized figures of the avant-garde, is one of the magazine's precursors. He anticipated the magazine's interest in the vernacular at a moment when most writers were looking to and adapting European models. Xul Solar created a precedent when he called for a "Neocriol" (neo-creole) language: a deliberate mixture of natural and artificial languages as seen in the text included in this anthology. But, in retrospect, he also fueled XUL's deliberate attack on language as handed down by the Spanish Royal Academy of Language in its attempt to regulate language usage since colonial times. An attack that was also directed against the appropriation of language that took place within the same official discourse of the same military government that promoted a long advertising campaign under the slogan "Silence is Health."

Oliverio Girondo is another of the magazine's most important precursors. Twenty years after his death, XUL dedicated an entire issue to him not simply because he belonged to an increasingly recognized canon but because his work could be seen as unique and transgressive at a time when "avant-garde" had already become a meaningless term. Girondo's last book, *En la masmédula* (1956), is one of Argentine poetry most challenging texts and XUL's editors regarded it as point of departure for a poetry in which the display of literary devices becomes an integral part of their own writing practice. *En la masmédula* had a similar influence on the editors as Gertrude Stein's work had on some of the American Language Poets. Both writers explore a poetics of exhaustion that invites few imitators but cannot be easily dismissed. The editors' interest in Girondo was also linked to their dedication to visual poetry. Many of the magazine's contributors were convinced that Girondo's work was a point of reference in the debate over whether it is possible to write poetry without an awareness of the linguistic and rhetorical devices which make writing possible. For many of XUL's readers, he is the poet who best represents the bridge to which the magazine's motto refers: **"XUL, Old and new sign."**

The editorial section—which has remained constant throughout the magazine's history and which was written both collectively and individually — consists of a running commentary on the community's institutional life. While it is true for many who published in XUL that formal experimentation could not be separated from political practice or, better yet, that it was their political practice, this activism did not exclude other kinds of commentary. Nor did XUL limit itself to publishing only one kind of material. In retrospect, the editorial section provides a frame for all the material published in the magazine. Many times the editorial focus was a case in point for the poetics proposed by the magazine and they actively embrace and work toward developing new cultural perspectives again making a case for the disassembling of our most dearest habits: subordination and authoritarism.

The translation of many of the poems in this anthology required a deconstruction of the mechanisms that made them possible in Spanish and the reconstruction of these same mechanisms in English. For example Jorge Lépore's "Ifulofnoforceps" forces long chains of portmanteau words in Spanish whose literal meaning in English is less interesting than the associative echoes they are capable of provoking. Originally done with cut-ups of the text that are typed on white paper with black ink and glued to black cardboard, these works want to function like a neon sign of the political and affective subconscious. The English version is a truly new poem, as though the original was but the instructions for a performance.

Other translations are the result of extensive correspondence or meetings with one or more readers and, in some cases, with the authors themselves. Molly

Weigel's translation of Jorge Perednik's poetry and K. A. Kopple's work on the editorials were done in close collaboration with the authors and editors. G. J. Racz's translation of Osvaldo Lamborghini's poem produced a detailed correspondence between the translator and myself. We talked extensively on the phone discussing the poems word by word and the difficulties of having to translate such an open body of work. The translator faced the challenge of not always being able to transpose into English certain constructions or the order of certain lines and having to translate the entire poem as a whole and not word by word.

Drawing attention to the different approaches to translation presented in this anthology as well as offering a bilingual edition is motivated by the desire to reveal the mechanisms of translation, a stance which is congruent with XUL's poetics.

For the editor who has tried to look at the same texts from two different cultural points of view, this anthology is itself an act of translation, an invention, once again, of what is Argentine and, to a certain extent, of what is American. The possible connections between north and south become evident in the affinities between XUL and L=a=n=g=u=a=g=e Magazine. To emphasize this connection, it is more attractive to make explicit those similarities between the two in order to create an encounter or to superimpose readings. This anthology was born as the result of that view and these encounters between texts and people.

ACKNOWLEDGEMENTS

Particular thanks to James Sherry the publisher of this book and Deborah Thomas in charge of the production of Roof Books, for their never failing faith in the project, the Poetics Program at Buffalo, and Charles Bernstein who supported and participated in the Poetics of the Americas conference which made it possible for the editor of XUL, Jorge Perednik, to come to the US during the spring of 1994. Heart felt thanks to each of the translators who put in hours of work to accomplish a very difficult job. This book exists because of their generosity and skills. Special thanks to Reinaldo Laddaga and K. A. Kopple for their insightful feedback during the two years it took to assemble this collection.

—*The editor*

The XUL Reader
AN ANTHOLOGY OF ARGENTINE POETRY
1980-1996

XUL: VARIATIONS ON THE NAME OF A MAGAZINE

by Jorge Santiago Perednik

tr. Molly Weigel

1980. What might the date signify? That year the first issue of the magazine XUL appeared. So, suddenly, in Argentina, under exceptional historical circumstances—the country in the grips of a military dictatorship and a terrorist politics that annhilated its subversive adversaries, that spread throughout the population, and produced tens of thousands of victims—XUL. The word offers itself as a curse or benediction, but applied to the name of a magazine it hoped to be an incantation against the epoch. It's hard to imagine what it means to live in terror; it could be said that those who had to were able to do so only through some kind—or various kinds—of conjuring, and that to live in terror with the constant consciousness of terror is unbearable. Whatever the individual means of conjuring these circumstances, including evading or denying them, the politics of terror marked its contemporaries and decades later continues in part to explain Argentine behavior.

Specifically, there was a generalized attitude after the end of the dictatorship: because the memory of such intense terror had become unbearable, because to relive it even in memory was to relive tragedy, a process began that might be called "repression of the experience of terror": the majority of Argentines, including intellectuals, involuntarily forgot this problem, leaving a recent part of history blank, and this particularly affected literature, criticism, and the teaching of literature, including, of course, the reading of the poems produced during that epoch (as well as the writing of those who came after).

Terror settles in people and affects them in unforeseen ways; in the case of Argentine poets, whatever they wrote about, even if they didn't intend to, they wrote about terror. Without the information, then, that certain poems were written during a regime of terror, a possible dimension of reading them is lost; if the fact that this experience existed and intersected the writing of the poems is repressed, access to multiple relations and a whole spectrum of interpretive paths is closed off to the reader. Removing terror from the terrorized is liberating, a relief; removing it from the history of a country that suffered it, not only avoiding thinking about it but also "forgetting" its occurrence, is to affirm that its effects continue to be felt and that the best kind of spell to place on them is denial.

The magazine carried the name of XUL for various reasons, among which euphony was neither the first nor the last. XUL is a word or sound that is pleasing to the ear—at least to this ear. And in this case the euphonic is also the foreign: xul is a grouping of sounds whose categorization as a word is doubtful, and even if it is accepted as such, it certainly does not belong to the Spanish language. It's a foreign sound in principle to almost all Spanish speakers, something that one doesn't know what it is or what it means. Also a word whose exact pronunciation is not self-evident: Csul, Sul, Zul, Shul? A street vendor of newspapers and magazines pronounced it Kul (confusing the "x" with a "k"), which might be taken as a compliment: a "cool" magazine.

In any case, as much for sound as for sense, it's a hard word to situate, and this is not foreign to a poetic proposition according to which the reader encounters the poem in a relationship of difficulty. In the first place, for the writer, deciding to write a poem and not another kind of writing is to embrace difficulty as one's task. Second, for the reader, reading the poem must always be an extremely difficult task, even when the poem presents itself as "simple," or especially in those cases—because simplicity is an appearance of the poem that is as complex as its opposite, or even more, especially when it manages, by hiding or negating the difficulty, to avoid its being read. On the other hand, it's a fact that the difficulties of a poem can't be established; they change even for a single reader through successive readings. This characteristic, once recognized, was deliberately used in poems, that is, incorporated as a feature of a poetics.

The design of the word XUL, written in capital letters, as in the magazine, also holds a programmatic interest: the X is a cross and also an enigma to discover; the U a line that returns on itself arriving at a new point, the L an abrupt swerve. In this name the sole manifesto of the magazine is drawn. The motto **Old and new sign**, for its part, expresses a way of looking at the sign that can become co-extensive with the poem and with literature, considering it old and new at the same time: supposing that in literature the new is always old and the old may be always new; postulating that there are no novelties and on the other hand that there never cease to be renovations. Inevitably everything was already made, and inevitably everything remakes itself, and is something else: any poetic return arrives at a new point, any repetition resists continuity, and any trajectory is in itself a change of direction.

To reclaim the old sign is also to reclaim tradition. The word "old" affirms something that cannot be appropriated, that time has made irreducibly foreign. The tradition itself cannot be appropriated, except partially, by means of a certain falsehood: the tradition that names itself is not the tradition, but only a kind of anthological edifice constructed with that which is continually under construction. And whether joining traditions or inventing their own, writers say to sustain these fictions that they need a game of antecedents who authorize their writings and allow them to be authority. This is a rhetorical task, which thus belongs in the realm of the persuasive: authors want to convince their virtual readers that their works are part of a certain legality: that they follow the norms—and even aim to be the paradigm—of an aesthetic code, ancient or new, but one with history, with antecedents of genius. What is certain, however, is that all these predecessors are posterior to the contemporaries, since these latter are the ones who invented them as predecessors. This is the paradox of literary tradition: for readers it's a game with history, with the fiction of a past that hides its fictitious character; for writers it's a futuristic game whose text presents itself temporally inverted.

There's also the possibility of a slightly more complicated game, which consists of considering that any poem, whatever its date of composition or publication, is contemporary. Girondo, Macedonio Fernández, Xul Solar, Borges, Juan L. Ortiz, Lamborghini, as synecdoches of their writings, are contemporary as long as they exist, because they are read and published and discussed in bars or on public transportation or in magazine articles, in present time. This list may be part of the tradition of XUL, of the framework of writings summarized and resumed in a peculiar way in the names of its authors: making tradition solely of contemporaneity, not fixing it in an institution or a monument, but rather unfastening it, considering it as something changing and alive.

Borges is contemporary with Perednik, not for Borges or Perednik, who encountered each other more than once in time and space, but for the others, who make them contemporary through their reading. Moreover, Borges is much more contemporary with Perednik for a single reader than Borges is with Borges for two extemporaneous readers, as he himself suggested in a famous story.

And here it seems fitting to mention one of the many contributions of Borges practiced by the poets who published in XUL: to show that everything, even the most complicated philosophical or literary problems, even biographies or politics, natural or exact sciences, plastic arts, film, publicity, psychology, social sciences, other texts, can, or better must, be treated literarily by writers. Everything may become part of literature because it is not a recipient but an attitude to which in principle nothing can be foreign. This attitude allows the poet to reclaim the rigorous use of reason, but also of passion. A reason that leans toward risks, passionate, and a passion that doesn't lead one astray from reason.

XUL is also one of the months in the Mayan calendar, the month that signifies the end of one era and the beginning of another. During this month the Spaniards arrived, which marked the end of the world for native civilization. Something ending and something beginning: in contrast to the aboriginal experience, living under the military dictatorship, XUL—understood as the end of one epoch and the beginning of another—was welcome. There were also literary desires for XUL during this epoch—for changing the poetic airs that people were breathing. The dominant poetics of the 60s and the beginning of the 70s had a simplified vision of reality—dual, with good and evil schematically localized—and correspondingly they used poetic forms of alleged simplicity. They also proposed a theoretical division between form and content, coherent in a way with their vision of reality: form was ill-regarded, suspicious, and content "good" insofar as it coincided with their political position. The poem was considered a vehicle for communicating messages that had to bombard readers and "awaken" them politically. For many poets who began to publish after 1976, forms that affect simplicity—including the dual, manichean vision of the world, the forced division between form and content, or the possibility of communicating messages that this offers—became insufficient and even dishonest. The complexity of the poems' artistic propositions was a response to a more complex vision of the world. This refigures the role of the reader, who is no longer a receptor of messages and of a truth emitted by the author, but rather a protagonist of the poem through his reading. And the role of the author was reconceived, removing his authority to guide or change the consciousness of others and even removing his power to decide the truth of the poem.

Poetics can be explosive or implosive; the explosive, whose movement goes out from the poem, in search of an author or the propagation of a meaning, and the implosive, in which the outside is attracted by a centripetal force, where the reader implodes toward the poem. An explosive poetics is in some way an expansive, conquering poetics, and this is what dominated in the 60s and the beginning of the 70s, when the desire was to use poetry for a political cause. And a poetics that inserted itself in the play of the spectacle also attempted this. Conquering the people, conquering the market, conquering the attention of the critical establishment—these provoked the epigraph of an editorial in the magazine: "Enough conquests, we're tired of winning." XUL is also the inversion of LUX, and we affirmed ourselves supporters of light against the long and terrible night we were living in. The epigraph to the first editorial reads "Sirbenet ni xul," which is "Lux in tenebris" backwards, or Latin for light in darkness. In relation to this it is also interesting to read the name XUL as a badly-written Roman numeral (XVL). The badly-written cipher breaks with any hope of cracking a code, a secure key for decipherment, and therefore discourages the hermetic expectations that may be placed in the poem. There's nothing farther from hermeticism than the poetics published in the magazine, whose task or proposition is not to establish secret meanings and hide them, but on the contrary to make signification possible by offering the reader work with signs, a work of reading. That is, the task of writing for these poets is not focused on converting poems into repositories of mystery, which is the property of the author and of a circle of initiates, but rather in operating with signs, with language, believing that meanings are not contained under lock and key within writings, nor instituted by the author, but rather that they must be constructed by the reader from texts and from language. On the other hand, the erroneous cipher, the badly written "sefer" (or book), proposes a writing that in its moment presents itself as "bad," of poor design, in the sense of separating itself from a dominant literary morality that likes to dictate what "the common good" is, or what is good. But there is no literary "good" or "bad." The writers' ethics are expressed in their writings and this is what sustains literature; this attitude of palming off an ethics onto literature itself, or onto poetry, of burying this text or that under "one can't" or "one mustn't," reveals the behavior of poetics that cannot sustain themselves from within. The ethics of the writers who published in XUL was based in risk and responsibility, separated from the institutionalized poetic "good," from that which was considered literarily "good," which in reality is the security of that which is the norm, to forge without restrictions and starting from whatever realm the adequate hows of the poem.

If it is certain that some poets placed the question of form and language at the center of their poetics, it is not because they wanted to, that is, a posteriori and by consequence of a programmatic decision, but rather because it was what they were able to do. One more time: the circumstances brought them to that point, to attempt poetic means that resisted the epoch. To coincide not in style but in the conviction that the means of resisting with art is through the how that the poems say: that in art what is said passes through the way of saying it. The poem is a significant form; in epochs of severe repression facility with the forms of saying permits escape from the vigilant gaze of the censor; as for interested readers, they become skilled: sharper, more critical. It can thus be concluded that the resistance of these poets was not the gesture of heroes, although a certain history might want to present it that way, but rather that it was their response to being placed in an impossible situation. If the expression "they walked the razor's edge" is appropriate, they created a poetry of boundaries, because they coudn't do anything else—not falling into the abyss on the one hand, and the abyss was the threat of dying at the hands of the repression, which killed many thousands of opponents; and not accepting, on the other hand, the security of firm ground, that is, poetic renunciation or temptation to the various forms of complacency.

During its existence the magazine went through an interesting experience: on one side necessity and on the other the difficulty that others had in cataloging the nature of the poetics found in its pages. The way these others found of resolving this problem was to use known categories. XUL was considered an organ of Russian formalism, of structuralism, of concrete poetry, of Tel Quel, of postmodernism, etc. It was believed, to develop an interesting example, that the magazine was the organ of an avant-garde poetic group, even when an editorial ridiculed the idea of the vanguard, the possibility that in literature someone is ahead of the rest, guiding them, or that a history of poetic progress may be conceived, so that the latest expressions are superior to what preceded them. Moreover the distinctive characteristics of an artistic vanguard were missing: there were no poetic manifestos, no name in common, and there wasn't even a group; on the contrary, there was a rejection of any idea of communal identification, and if there were concurrences in the writings of different poets, this was not owing to any agreement prior or exterior to the poems themselves, nor to a submission to an instituted poetic code; on the contrary, a common unity among poets was the cause of differing poetics, since writing is done by different individuals and since the poem does not deserve to be restricted by boundaries or classifications.

In reality, the concept of a vanguard, like so many other concepts, is not a stimulus or trigger but rather an imposition, because it is the fruit of a certain critical desperation. Whenever phenomena occur in the terrain of art that escape the predictability of a history of comfortable development, these all-encompassing critical sophistries appear. Concepts like the vanguard, postmodernism, etc., must be strong in order to hide their poverty, their incapacity. Since they are ill-adapted to explain that which is varied, complex, contradictory, and in no way a unique occurrence, these concepts superimpose on it a unitary hypothesis, a hypostasis that occupies its place with a generalized intention. The result goes against art: it erases the individuality of each act and its differences from the rest. For example, Bauhaus doesn't have much to do with Dada, even though both are grouped under the same explanatory category. What does this process accomplish? —To tranquilize critical thinking, making it think that with this concept it is becoming conscious of artistic reality. To tranquilize assuring that there's nothing more to think, that the thinkable has already been expressed.

What should have been first remains for the last: XUL, the name of the magazine, was an homage to Xul Solar, a singularly complex individual, writer among many other things, although he was known mainly as one of the principal plastic artists of Argentina. Borges said of Solar:

> A man well-versed in all the disciplines, seeker after arcana, father of writings, of languages, of utopias, of mythologies, guest of hells and heavens, pan-chessplayer and astrologer, perfecter of indulgent irony and generous friendship, Xul Solar is, of our few events, one of the most singular. Xul believed that humans too have a mission to recreate. . . . In the face of silence or smiles, Xul embraced the destiny of proposing a system of universal reforms. He wanted to recreate the religions, astrology, math, society, numeration, writing, vocabulary, the arts, the musical instruments, and toys. He premeditated two languages. One, a creole, was American Spanish, quickened, exalted, and multiplied; the other, a pan-language, whose words had their own definitions according to the value of the letters, in the manner of the analytical language of John Wilkins. A similar idea to a semicircular keyboard, reducing the pianist's labor, and that always inconclusive and ever more complicated pan-game that, under the umbrella of chess, embraced many disciplines and could be played on various planes. All this in Buenos Aires, land of imitative innovators and reliable mirrors. Predictably the utopias of Xul Solar failed, but the failure is ours, not his. We didn't know how to deserve him.

The magazine XUL, in the manner of an inverted LUX, existed to illuminate a region of the stage that was there but that could not be seen. It published poetry, scandalous during its time, that nobody dared to publish, and unknown authors that would soon be considered the protagonists of their age. It believed that the strongest and most interesting voice in poetry is that which speaks by operating, and by being operated on, by, and with language. It discovered for its country's literature a new universe, and as with all discoveries, it invented it. To embody a time and space in Argentine poetry a simple recourse was enough: to give room to that chosen one that had no place.

This essay was written especially for this anthology.

THE PREDECESSORS

Martín Fierro

(excerpt)

by José Hernández

Now I shall begin to sing
to the rhythm of the guitar,
for a man who cannot rest
from pain so extraordinary,
like a bird so solitary
comforts himself with song.

I ask the saints in heaven
to assist me in my thinking,
I ask them at this moment
in which I am going to sing my story
to refreshen my memory,
and clarify my understanding.

Come saints, with your miracles,
come all of you to my aid,
because my tongue is twisting,
and my sight growing dim—
I beg my God to help me
at such a difficult time.

Martín Fierro by José Hernández (XUL #4 p.4)
Aquí me pongo a cantar\al compás de la vigüela,\que al hombre que lo desvela\una pena extraordinaria\como el ave solitaria\con el cantar se consuela.\\Pido a los santos del cielo\que ayuden mi pensamiento\les pido en este momento\que voy a cantar mi historia\me refresquen la memoria\ y aclaren mi entendimiento.\\Vengan Santos milagrosos\vengan todos en mi ayuda\que la lengua se me añuda\y se me turba la vista\pido a mi Dios que me asista\en una ocasión tan ruda.

I have seen many singers
whose fame was well won,
and after they've achieved it
they can't keep it up—
it's as if they'd tired in the trial runs
without ever starting the race.

But where another criollo goes
Martín Fierro will go to:
there's nothing sets him back,
even ghosts don't scare him,
and since everybody sings
I want to sing also.

Singing I'll die,
singing they'll bury me,
and singing I'll arive
at the Eternal Father's feet—
out of my mother's womb I came
into this world to sing.

Yo he visto muchos cantores,\con famas bien obtenidas,\y que después de alquiridas\no las quieren sustentar\parece que sin largar\se cansaron en partidas.\\Mas ande otro criollo pasa\Martín Fierro ha de pasar\nada lo hace recular\ni los fantasmas lo espantan\y dende que todos canten\yo también quiero cantar.\\Cantando me he de morir,\cantando me han de enterrar,\y cantando he de llegar\al pie del Eterno Padre\dende el vientre de mi madre\vine a este mundo a cantar.

Scarecrow

by Oliverio Girondo

tr. Molly Weigel

```
                    I   know   nothing
                    You know nothing
                    He knows nothing
                    She knows nothing
                    One knows nothing
                    They know nothing
                  We   know   nothing
    The  disorientation  of  my  generation  has  its
   explanation  in  the  administration  of  our  education,
  whose  idealization  of  action  was—without  question!—
        a  mystification,  in  contradiction
        to  our  predilection  for  medi-
        tation,  contemplation,  and
        masturbation.  (Guttural,  as
        gutturally  as  possible.)
        I  believe  I  believe  in
        what  I  believe  I  don't
        believe.  And  I  believe
        I  don't  believe  in
        what  I  believe
        I  believe.
        "Songofthefrogs"
        And  And  Is     Is   And  And
         I    I    it     it    I    I
          a   de   there?  yon   a   de
        scend scend  It    der? scend scend
         up  down   is      It   up  down
         the  the   not     Is   the  the
         es   es     a      not  es   es
         ca   ca    round   here ca   ca
         la   la     !       !   la   la
        tor!... tor!...          tor!...  tor!...
```

Espantapájaros by Oliverio Girondo (XUL #6 p.31)
Yo no sé nada\Tú no sabes nada\Ud. no sabe nada\Él no sabe nada\Ellos no saben
nada\Ellas no saben nada\Uds. no saben nada\Nosotros no sabemos nada\\La desori-
entación de mi generación tiene su\explicación en la dirección de nuestra educación,\cuya
idealización de la acción, era -¡sin discusión!-\una mistificación, en contradicción\con
nuestra propensión a la medi-\tación, a la contemplación y a la\masturbación. (Gutural,lo
más\guturalmente que se pueda.) \Creo que creo en lo que\creo que no creo. Y creo\que
no creo en lo\que creo que creo.\"Cantar de las ranas"\\¡Y ¡Y ¿A ¿A ¡Y ¡Y\su ba llí
llá su ba\bo jo es es bo jo\las las tá? tá? las las\es es ¡A ¡A es es\ca ca quí cá
ca ca\le le no no le le\ras ras es es ras ras\arri aba tá tá arri aba\ba! jo! !... !...
ba! jo!...

3

Poem
Xul Solar

This Hades is fluid, almist, no roof, no floor, redhaired, color in sunshut eyes, stirred in endotempest, whirlpools, waves, and boiling. In its clots n foam dismultitumans float passivao, disparkle, therz also solos, adults, kidoids, n they pergleam softao.

Transpenseen ghostliao, the houses n people n soil of a solid terri citi have nothing to do withis Hell, which is nao thereal.

This whole dense redheaded region selfmountains roun big hollo or bottomless valley of bluegray air, where it floes in dark winds, with uproarians n other lone umans, avoid n globoid. Here it floes more oop. N yon the solid city n its populas go on ghostliao.

Later I pass on to a better life, gray silver. Yere many groups lovefloat loosao processioning or thinking reunited. Yere clouds row with gray kiosks—of mother of pearl, metal, felt—with pensors circumseated.

Sloao I find myselfe in a slight kelestal sky. Its disposition is afternoon summeri, cloudii.

Plants zigzag one by one biomove and hum. Ther color lovaries from garnet to rosy. They r over floatislope of da same denser air, undspersing. Here juxtafly boids like speck eggs, not with wings, but with many ribbons.

"Poem by Xul Solar (XUL #1 p.21)
Es un Hades fluido, casi vapor, sin cielo, sin suelo, rufo, color en ojos cérrados so el sol agítado en endotempestá, vórtices, ondas y hervor. En sus grumos i espumas dismultitú omes flotan pasivue, disdestellan, hai también solos, mayores, péjoides, i perluzen suavue.\\Se transpenvén fantasmue las casas i gente i suelo de una ciudá sólida terri, sin ningún rapor con este Hades, qes aora lô real.\\Toda esta región rufa densa se montona redor gran hueco ho valle sin fondo, de aire azul gris, do floto en vientos oscuros, con polvareda gente, i otros omes solos ávoides i globoides. Aqí se flota más upa. I siga fantasmue la ciudá sólida yu i su pópulo.\\Paso luego a mejor vida, gris plata. Yi qierflotan flojue muchos grupos, procesionan o pensan reúnidos. Yi bogan nubes con qioscos grises —de nácar, metal, fieltro—con pénsores circunsiéntados.\\Lentue me hallo en cielo leve ciéleste. Su ánimo es de tarde verani, niebli.\\Plantas de a un zigzag se biomuevan i canturrian. Xu color qiervaría de granate a róseo. Están sobrs loma floti del mismo aire mas denso, soesfúminse. Yi yuxtavuelan pájaros como huevos pintos, no con alas, sino con muchas cintas.

Nex therz many color columns, baseless, supporting cloud roof: is temple floati in which many pray. When zey theocoexalt zey inflate, zer auras vitaradiate, suchao zat zey raize ze cloud roof an circumseparate ze columns, an everysing fervienlarges n saintgleams.

Nex therz wide obelisk or tower, that swéz from its floatifloppi base. Its first floor, of stonebooks, mudbooks on top, woodbooks on top, cylinder books on top, the top, books. Almost lyk a house of cards, bristling with paper ribbons n banderols, periflown with letterswarms flyao, juxtasurrounded by perhaps wandermunching studenti. Inna lil bit of floor floati, many dream, zer mersed.

I float I go yonderfarre. Deeping in a plurmutacolor fog I see ceety. Thees biopalaces n biohovels, of framework n I theenk. They pertransform, grow or shreenk; now they r pillars n archframes n cupolas, now plain phosphiplastered walls, now they quake weeth pseudocrystal scaffolding. They shift, rise, seenk, interpenetrate, separate, n rejoicetera.

Houses ther r that burn, flame oop, but they don't self-destruct, they rather selfconstruct-um. Der fire is life, n da greater da boining, da more palace senwidens n grows. Houses ther r that infect set fire to the nébors that idem idem, n thus néborhoods expand. Ther people lykwise coflame n coloom: this must be the cause burni, by pensiardor.

Houses ther r that ferviboil until they blow up lyk a bomb, a geyser, or smoke; but they d'ont self-destruct-um, they circumreselfconstruct; ther

Otrur hai muchas columnas color, sin suelo, qe sostienen nube techo: es templo floti en qe oran muchos. Cuando se teocoexaltan se hinchan, xus auras irradian vita, talue qe alzan la nube techo i circunseparan las columnas, i todo se ferviagranda i sanluze.\\Otrur hai obelisco ancho ho torre, bambolea por su base flotifloja. Su primer piso, de libros piedra, encima libros barro, encima libros leña, encima libros rollo, la cima libros. Casi como torre naipes, erízada de cintas papel i banderolas, perivuélada de letrienjambres moscue, yuxtarodeada de qizás mangente vaga estudi. En el poco suelo floti sueñan muchos, yi mérgidos.\\Floto voi allén lejos. Hónduer en niebla plurcambicolor veo ciudá. Sas biopalacias y biochozas, de armazón i pienso. Se pertransforman, se agrandan o achican; ya son de postes i cimbras i cúpulas, ya de muros lisos en parches fosfi, ya pululan en biocúmulos, ya temblequean de andamios seudocristal. Se desplazan, suben, se hunden, se interpenetran, se sepa i réidem.\\Casas hai qe arden, flamean upa, pero no se destruyen, se ñe construyen más. Xu fuego es vita, i a mayor incendio, más palacio senancha i crece. Casas hai qe contagian incendian a las vecinas qe ídem ídem, i así sextiendan los barrios. Xu yi gente también, coflamea i se coabulta: debe ser ella la causa fuegui, por pensiardor.\\Casas hai qe fervihiervan hasta qe revientan como bomba ho geiser o humo; pero no se ñe destruyen, se circunreconstruyen; xas bits n pieces fervigrow in faraway subsidiaries that finally growjoin, dispile tower morrenmore, on circumbarrens lessenless.

Houses ther r that suigrow in evri direkshun, skewpi, horizily, juxto, oop, fat; n they buzz, squeak, creak, dispeak.

Houses ther r that atrophy and shrink until they r seen no mor, when ther people diehatch inna better life inna better sky.

Houses ther r of illusion on smokehills; they altervanish.

So I embrace the soil of this citi, that wichis a cloudgathering, wichis several vague titans floatireclining.

Great sleeves or tubes circumset out-um for the vacuum: they might be sewers or suckers, I do'nt know.

N over that ceety ther ees other ceety, backward, sullen, dark n slow that lives n grows juxto, n its people too. The nadir is deep, sullen, dark, foggi: maybe the hommeworld, some great wasteland.

I review the other city oop. Colonnades like centipedes travell in distrides. They r rigid disciples, carrying dometeachers with wide roofly robes. Tumbled in suihappy skyrabble, lovi-turvy in fog and sketches and clots of thot: gelatine menti. They go farre, into the vacuum.

I see zerz several very pily pagodas of just bookes, zat zer many readers incorpor-ate: they don't read, but rather vitisuck science n sophy.

trozos fervicrecen en sucursales lejos qe alfín se crecijuntan, dismontón torre mahimás, sobre circumbaldío menoimenos.\\Casas hai qe suicrecen en todo séntido, sesgüe, horizue, yuso, upa, gordue; i zumban, chirrian, crujen, disparlan.\\Casas hai que se atrofian i encojen hasta no verse más, cuando xa gente muertinace a mejor vida en mejor cielo.\\Casas hai de ilusión sobre cerros humo: se cambipierden.\\Entonces abarco el suelo desa ciudad, el qes una sûnnube, qes varios titanes vagos flotiacuéstados.\\Grandes mangas o tubos ñe circunsalgan a lo vacuo: serian cloacas o chúpores, no sé.\\I so esa ciudá hai otra ciudá'l revés, hosca, oscura i lenta qe vive i crece yuso, i sa gente también. El nadir es hondo, hosco, oscuro, brúmoso: qizás el manmundo, algún gran yermo.\\Reveo la otra ciudá upa. Columnatas como cienpiés viaján a distrancos. Son discípulos tiesos, llevan maestros cúpulas, de rópaje ancho techue. A tumbos sobre chusma cieli suifeliz, qierrevuelta en bruma i cuágulos i bocetos de pienso: gelatina menti. Van a lejos, a lô vacuo.\\Veo hai algunas mui moles pagodas de solos libros, qe se incuerpan a xus tantos léctores—qe no leen, masbién vitichupan ciencia i sofia.

Bawlings propagate, undulate in all linguages n many others possible. N these letterswarms, n glyftangles, n disfonetix n copluracents, like a bunch of lovesmokes, separate or join, countermove or subside, in order or not, form n reform meaning n argu, always neo.

Stars, little suns, moons, moonlets, lightning bugs, lanterns, lites, lusters; anywhere they get lifentangled in the city they constellate n disconstellate, burn themselves, go out, mixshine, rain, fly.

It's a perflux n reflux of breeze n fluid n blast n sounds n smellsteam; the lite perchanges, in splendor color, heat, chiaroscuros, in soul.

Already gonetired, I grow dazed n forget, dissee.

Everything pales, n erases itself. Already it seems I'm entering a greater sky th'ats another nite, that later is more nite, that is more, deep solid black theonite, that I manfear n mistilov; ther I would exdizolv.

But something vaguimmense comes between me n the theonite; like plurcolored gas. It becomes more defined, n i'ts an indefinite godhombre, skydiameter. Its head across me, its feet before me, in the counterhorizon, n its hands over me, fiftinihookpointi, r orange; its clothing, indecisive cambicolor in patches.

Above its head nao flowers a white flower lite. Its scarlet heart radiates pink lite, its garnet pudenda's onlylite.

I feel as if I'm entering the godhombre, which transports me yere.

But already the call of this Earth from yon oppresses my breast bodii; n I return to myself quite perpenao.

Sexpandan, ondulan voceríos de todas las linguas i de muchas otras pósibles. I xas enjambres letras, i marañas glifos, i disfonéticas i copluracentos, como muchos qierhumos, se apartan o juntan, se contramueven o aqietan, en orden o no, forman, reforman séntido i argu siempre neo.\\Estrellas, sólcitos, lunas, lúnulas, luciérnagas, linternas, luces, lustres; doqier se vidienredan a la ciudá se constelan i disconstelan, se qeman, se apagan, cholucen, llueven, vuelan.\\Es un perflujo i reflujo de brisa i flúido i ráfaga i sones i humos olor; la luz percambia, en lampos color, calor, claroscuros, en ánimo.\\Yo ya veicánsado me aturdo i olvido, disveo.\\Todo palidece, i se borra. Ya parece qentro a mayor cielo qes otra noche, qes luego más noche, qes más, teonoche honda sólida negra, qe mantemo i mistiamo; yo me yi exdisolverío.\\Pero algo vago inmenso se interpone'ntre mi i lo teonoche; como gas plurcolor. Se define más, i es un mandivo indefinido, cielidiámetro. Su testa tras mî, sus pies ante mî, en el contrahorizonte, i sus manos sobre mî, ganchipuntitóqinse, son oranje; su rópaje, cambicolor indeciso en parches.\\Sobre su testa florece aora flor luz blanca. Su cuore punzó irradia luz rósea, su pudenda granate's sólodeluz.\\Sento como qentro al mandivo, qe me yi arrobo.\\Pero ya la llámada desta Terra desde yu me oprime'l pecho cuerpi; i vuelvo a mî mui perpenue.

The Most Amusing Song of the Devil (excerpt)

(a prose work half in verse, no joke...)

by Osvaldo Lamborghini

tr. G. J. Racz

Hamlet, that Creole pip,
and the Ghost of his dead Father:
I've been forced to make a slip.
Revenge...!

Oh chilly Song of the Garnett
On his Cross each variant word
And one and Soup and Sam
Still forward

       a!
b be nd me ov er
r re am me rov er
very deserted
be nd me ov er
I'll sing it ov er and ov er

it's the truth
though strongly asserted!

and forward!
Devil!
Oh Devils!
Song of the Devil!
The Amusing

IT'S MY LIFE!

Song of the Devil!

La Divertidisima Canción Del Diantre
(obra en prosa y medio en verso, sin chanza...) by Osvaldo Lamborghini (XUL#11 p.20)
Oh friolenta Canción del Garnett\En su Cruz cada variante\Y una y Sopa y Sam\Más ade-
lante\¡a!\e éncu léme\a ángu léme\muy desierto\en cu le mé\yo can ta ré\¡es verdad!\¡es
cierto!\¡y adelante!\¡Diantre!\¡Oh Diantres!\¡Canción del Diantre!\La Divertida\¡ES MI
VIDA!\Canción del Diantre

THE DEVIL YOU S
AY
    ???!!!

don't be so gutu

                —I'll write you up in my book—

if you're here

                —and not in the nook—

Unforgivable
the word sun glow
the word sunk low
unforgivable
but the silence is binding

                —attention: the Aga Muffin is speaking—

AND SPACE
(why the capitals?)
devil on top of devil
and ass and devil and patience
(slow the pace)
and the sun glow sunk low
and before before in front of all
with clearsightedness

                    OF THE COLD
                    BIRTH OF TERROR

and still before

                    before!
                    before!
                    before!

¡¡¡¡¡DIANTR\EH\?????\no seas tan gutu\—que yo te ficho—\si estás aquí\—y no en el nicho—\Sin perdón\la palabra un día\la palabra hundía\sin perdón\pero el silencio ata\—atención: habla el Atha Philtrafa-\Y ESPACIO\(¿por qué mayúsculas?)\diantre sobre diantre\y culo y diantre y paciencia\(más despacio)\y un día hundía\y antes y antes y delante\y en videncia\DEL FRIO\PARTO DEL TERROR\y todavía antes\¡antes!\ ¡antes!\¡antes!

9

I despise
Mia
Moa my own price!
like the tele tells you tele the vision
I remember all too well!
crazy alarming clock!
with its tick-tock!

the devil!

I suffer amnesia in no wise
but did I pay my own price?
Moa Mia
Where to go? A ir France?
be frantic and go wing it?
and should I

should I sing it?
fine!
the devil take it!

: OH MOST AMUSING
SONG OF THE DEVIL

Argentina is done,
The Old Dead Mare!
They knock quickly my beloved
fatherland Moa
Mia
on our doors over here

Moa Mia please!
it's the police!
it's the police!
it's the police!

¡desprecio\Mia\Moa mi precio!\como tele te lo dice el tele el vizor\¡bien que me
acuerdo!\¡loco y reloj!\¡despertador!\¡*diantre!*\no me amnesio\ ¿pero pagué mi
precio?\Moa Mia\¿Adónde ir? ¿A ir France?\¿pero del ir ante?\¿y que yo*yo la
cante?*\¡*bueno!*\¡*diantre*: OH DIVERTIDISIMA\CANCION DEL DIANTRE\
¡Argentina!\¡Yegua Muerta!\Rápido querida\patria Moa\Mia\llaman a la puerta*¡Moa
Mia!**¡es la policía!**¡es la policía!**¡es la policía!*

10

Save your damn skin, if it's not worth losing
(how amusing!)
it's the police!
it's the police!
And Ascasubi founded
the *Teatro Colón*
Call me already
(what for? don't call me)
all ready
           —CALL ME...!—
yoke the neck firmly

                and there are no limbos
                oh throat-slashers

now don't you forget me
to Mia
Oh Amusing
Song of the Devil

                There is flesh
                and there is blood
                and there is chocolate
                thick as mud
                sans gré
                sans gré

And your two halves
are tremendous

¡Hay que salvar la puta vida!\(¡divertida!)\¡es la policía!\¡es la policía!\Y Ascasubi que fundó\el Teatro Colón.\Y ya me\(no llame ¿para qué?)\ya me...\-¡LLAME. . . !-\yugan el cogote\y *no hay limbos\oh degolladores*\pero no me olvides\tú a Mia\Oh Divertida\Canción del Diantre\\Hay carne\y hay hueso\y hay chocolate\bien espeso\san gré\san gré\\Y son tremendas

Juana Blanco
so equal:
and now here lies you.

> Lo Garnett
> Mo Garnett
> Bo Garnett

Garnetts: are there Garnetts?
The Devil!
What about the vultures?
And the tips of hairs?
And the green fields where they lay
(this has nothing to do with the tero)
the guliguli pic pic on the eggs?
And the amusing
song of the devil?
Now here lies you

This mate tastes really bad
down to (that will do!)
the bottom of the cup
(I no longer listen up)
its taste is rather bitter and

> —*Is it the bitter end?*

it's the bitter end!
(calm: peace, it's the bitter end)
oh amusing
song of the devil
how our lives seem
to end up in the trash

Juana Blanco\tus dos mitades\tan iguales:\ahora yaces.\Lo Garnett\Mo Garnett\Bo Garnett\Garnetts:¿hay Garnetts?\¡Diantre!\¿Y los caranchos?\¿Y la punta de los pelos?\¿Y los campitos donde ponen\(y nada que ver el tero)\la guliguli pic pic en los huevos?\¿Y la divertida\canción del diantre?\Ahora yaces\\Qué mal sabe el mate\y hasta (¡basta!)\el pucho\(ya no escucho)\tiene un gusto acre\-¿*Es lo más acre?*\¡es la masacre!\(calma: paz, es la masacre)\oh divertida\canción del diantre\cómo caen las vidas\tan al pedo

lightning flash
like wax letter-sealant

AND,

in the final poem, without excruciating pain
although, Neibis, what agony it was, what a finale...
So finally, here,
the bird
or the trees that dream and dream
like animals
or those two halves
here lies you:
which poem was that?

the bird, hum,
the flower
both up at the sun's first ray
at dawn
they exh alae
they flutter on
Ann

And I am
and can explain it
without horror

AND,

Lord Garnett

al relámpago\como lacre\\Y,\\en el poema final, sin agonías\si bien, Neibis, qué agonía, qué final...\Si final, aquí,\el pájaro\o los árboles que sueñan y sueñan\como animales\o las dos mitades\yaces:\¿qué poema?\\el pájaro, hum,\la flor\despiertos al primer rayo\al amanecer\ex alan\aletean\Ann\\Y yo soy\y sin horror\puedo explicarlo\\Y,\Lord Garnett

Monsieur Garnett
Obispo
BispoShop Garnett,

congratulations

Thank you for the feast of meat
and all the free-flowing wine.
Ah, and
the devil! I almost forgot
thank you
thank you very much
now here lies you
on account of the Amusing
song: Song of the Devil
Now it's time to sleep it off
to sleep off the void
and await one's fate

Oh, devil!...
Mia Moa, the peon   *(I quote)*
his childish mischief
ran off with the guitar

                    Inland
                    He rides
                    On his blossom horse
                    Again the Desert site
                    Do I wake
                    or write?

Monsieur Garnett\Obispo\BispoShop Garnett,\\felicitaciones\\Gracias por la carneada\y el
abundante coperío. Ah, y\¡diantre! me olvidaba\gracias\muchas gracias\ahora yaces\por la
Divertida\ canción: Canción del Diantre\Ahora hay que dormir la mona\y la nada\y esperar
la suerte\\¡Oh, diantre!...\Mia Moa, el peón *(cito)*\su travesura de pibe\escapó con la guitar-
ra\Tierra adentro\Allá va\En el overo\Otra vez el Desierto\¿Estoy escribiendo\o estoy
despierto?

14

Forward, for words yearning
In these lonely spaces
Burning
In these discreet...silences...
Either fields of God
/or of the Foetus/
/Ogival/
/Water, now-here lies you/
/Wawalala...

Oh Living
Concluded
Oh amusing
Song of the Devil
Concluded
OH MOST AMUSING SONG OF THE DEVIL!!!!!

Adelante, va a delante\En esas soledades\Anhelantes\En esos silencios...discretos...\O campos de Dios\/o del Feto/\/Ojival/\ /Agua, ahora yaces/\/Gualala...\\Oh Vida\Terminada\Oh divertida\Canción del Diantre\Terminada\¡¡¡¡¡OH DIVERTIDISIMA CANCION DEL DIANTRE!!!!!

15

THE POEMS

Four poems
by Leonardo Scolnick

tr. G. J. Racz

1
Aviary ribcages
belly on breast
and genitals manifold

are entirely firmly
loaded
with projects and works

they're used to moaning about hypertrophic mothers
like Leda
between the darkness and the legs
of linen tablecloths

ribcages their ribcages
fists that strike their own

but in the supreme moment
when what is attained so bizarrely
drops
along with flowered underpants
its tenacious fight

Cuatro poemas by Leonardo Scolnick (XUL #1 p.27)
1\Costillares de avería\con panza en pecho\y múltiples genitales\\son totalmente dura-
mente\enteros\de proyectos y obras\\suelen gemir de madres hipertróficas\como Leda\entre
la oscuridad y las piernas\de los manteles de hilo\\costillares sus costillares\puños que gol-
pean los suyos\\pero en el instante supremo\cuando lo conseguido tan bizarramente\baja
con sus calzoncillitos floreados\su tenaz lucha

Ah how conscientious he looks
cleaning
so very clean

before him who is good
he who has affection aplenty
the clown on his own time

2
Heading home again:

The charnel houses flourish
a dignity never forgotten
is dispelled with the odor
gripping the small hand
the girl apple of our eyes suffocates

now they predominate
the instinct of preserving
the
  accumulated
              lives
                    of other
selves
our groping in the darkness
slipping away
                more falls
on one side than the other
what is this party we are attending?!
Oh foul-smelling needle hairy womb

Ay qué esmerado se lo ve\limpiando\limpísimo\frente al que es bueno\el que tiene afecto a raudales\el payaso sin horario\\2\La vuelta al hogar\\Florecen los osarios\dignidad que nunca olvidada\se disipa con el olor\apretando la manita\la niña de los ojos se sofoca\\es la época en que priman\el instinto de conservación\de la\vida\ de los\otros\acumulada\la nuestra tantea en la oscuridad\ escurrirse\más cae\en un lado de los dos\¡¿qué es esta fiesta en que participamos?!

shiny bald head of Mussolini's masseur who drinks wine
straight from your conch
blue is where they keep the pinhole
that cannot be seen when folded in upon itself
that presses the button on the doll
I am
and it will say strange things monsters parents who appear
dreams where games mix in
there is a game one must not play

3
One succeeds through repetition
in placing the thingy within
where the sacred object lies
the world reduced at the urgings of height
we play at raising muscle and bone a ruminant beast
packs up its faded-blond lassitude
brightness of our age
photos of the baby girl's smile
the concert in a minor key repeats when truly seen
a false note, a false note

Oh agujita maloliente vientre peludo\lustrosa la calva del masajista de Mussolini que toma
vino\derecho de tu concha\azul es donde guardan el agujerito\que no se puede mirar si
doblada sobre sí misma\apreta el botón de la muñeca\que soy yo\y habla cosas raras mons-
truos padres que aparecen\sueños donde se mezclan los juegos\hay un juego que no hay
que jugar\\3\Se logra por repetición\meter el coso por dentro\en que está la cosa
sagrada\reducido el mundo a instancias de la altura\jugamos a levantar el hueso y el múscu-
lo bestia rumiante\empaca su lasitud de rubia desteñida\brillo de nuestra edad\fotos de la
risa de la nena\repite el concierto en menor que visto en verdad\ desafina, desafina

4
a stampeding mob
digests its song which is not followed
to grief but to the heart in my breast
soft are the fangs that squeeze until they draw blood
and seeing the day like a trumpet-blare of clarity straining
to empty the eyes
fear sits upon a small straw chair
and embraces its body
wishing neither to pardon
nor elevate the word above the trembling
sharp the fangs that shatter the mandible
this really may be said, truly surely
of course

4\turba de estampidas\digiere su canto y es que no se sigue\hasta el duelo sino hasta el corazón de mi pecho\blandos los colmillos de apretar hasta sangrar\y ver el día como un trompeteo de claridad pujando\por vaciar los ojos\el miedo se sienta en una sillita de paja\y se abraza a su cuerpo\no quiere perdonar\ni quiere levantar la palabra sobre el temblor\agudos los colmillos que rompen la mandíbula\realmente se puede decir, en verdad claro\por supuesto

(Like a madwoman sewing...)

by Laura Klein

tr. Molly Weigel

like a madwoman sewing in front
of a dry window
and would shield the eye from seeing
as if there were pure something
to defend and this thing its store
defined itself falling into silence
by ineffable carelessness or history

(Como loca que cose. . .) by Laura Klein (XUL #2 p.23)
como loca que cose frente\a una ventana seca\y defendiera el ojo de mirar\por si puras
hubiera algo\que guardar y éste su acervo\defínese cayendo al silencio\por descuido inefa-
ble o historia.

Hardnesses

by Laura Klein

We rather watched
the house,
      the ugly,
        the good
          the trap,
            the house
with spines of steam
and our

but nothing was lacking
that furious time
and a blazing
          was enough
          another boat burned
          and until when.

Durezas by Laura Klein
Nosotros más miramos la casa,\la fea,\la buena\la trampa,\la casa\con espinas de vapor\y
nuestra\\pero nada hacía falta\esa rabiosa vez\y bastó\un fulgor\otra nave quemada\y hasta
cuándo.

(Of collateral all...)

by Laura Klein

tr. Molly Weigel

**it's a bellyful, of a thousand makeovers
on the empty coasts...**

of collateral all reality

a sweet minus: the heart

step by baby step is a bundle
only
      in August
the thing was to kill and correct
kill and collect the eyes don't know
there was a seasoning gunfire sad heads
the material of enormous books
under duress

the hand imprisoned in the mouth
squeezes words
hits takes gelds the best

at the party they keep having
until dawn

oh venture
laughter and hangover mix
until dawn.

(De fianzas la toda. . .) by Laura Klein
es un hartazgo, de mil afeites en las costas vacías . .\de fianzas la toda realidad\\un dulce
menos: el corazón\\pasito a paso que es un bulto\sólo\en agosto\la cosa fue matar y corre-
gir\matar y colegir que los ojos no saben\hubo un fogueo cabezas tristes\el material de
libros enormes\bajo pena\\la mano presa en la boca\aprieta palabras\pega toma capa lo
mejor\\en la fiesta siguen dando\hasta la madrugada\\oh ventura\mézclanse risa y
resaca\hasta las madrugadas,

(By the Same Pencilstroke...)

by Laura Klein

tr. Molly Weigel

by the same pencilstroke they erase
head of ends or hand in white
it's the same

they must be fearsome in the park alone
when the quiet in ambush

strange when they push ladies in the sea

calm down country and those who dance
play servant: nobody
had anything nobody spoke nobody was
with lowered eyes without parody or any grimace
there in the light

they raise fists and there's no case
they think thicken and it's not
better to sleep like an animal

on the sons they enter in a rage

dress in gold or fuzz

they must be fearsome when

they push ladies in the sea.

(Del mismo plumetazo. . .) by Laura Klein
del mismo plumetazo borran\cabeza de finales o mano en blanco\es igual \\han de ser temi-
bles en el parque solo\cuando la quieta acecha\\extraños cuando empujan damas al
mar\\cálmese el país y los que bailan\hagan de sirvientes: nadie\tuvo nada ni habló es que
nadie estuvo\con los ojos bajos sin parodia ni gesto\alguno hubo en la luz\\alzan el puño y
no hay caso\creen crecen y no\vale dormir como animal\\sobre los hijos entran a furia\\se
visten de plata o pelusa\\han de ser temibles cuando\\empujan damas al mar.

Tuyú

by Néstor Perlongher

tr. Molly Weigel

History, is it a language?
Does this language have to do with the language of history
or with the history of language/
where it stuttered/
Does it have to do with this verse?
living tongues licking dead tongues
tongues rotting like socks
tongues, lingering, fungous
this language of history/ which history?
if the long history of the tongue isn't taken as a story

They tell it
in a galley:

Miz Rudecinda
didn't the riding gear sprinkle the soul?
didn't the screamer bird scare itself?

(Melted gauchos, with their cow tongues, with their clubs
with their yokes and their silver coin belts
melted gaucho: he digs his spurs into the—melted—back
of the tongue, as if trapped in a rabbit warren)

Tuyú by Néstor Perlongher (XUL #2 p.26)
La historia, es un lenguaje?\Tiene que ver este lenguaje con el lenguaje de la historia\o con
la historia del lenguaje /\en donde balbuceó /\tiene que ver con este verso?\lenguas vivas
lamiendo lenguas muertas\lenguas menguadas como medias\lenguas, luengas, fungosas:\
este lenguaje de la historia / cuál historia?\si no se tiene por historia la larga historia de la
lengua\\Cuentan\en un fogón:\\Ña-Rudecinda\no roció el apero el ánima?\no se hizo jabón
el chajá?\\(Gauchos fundidos, con sus lenguas de vaca, con sus trancas\con sus coyundas y
sus rastras\Gaucho fundido: él clava sus espuelas en el dorso — fundido —\de la lengua,
como atrapado en una vizcachera)

A few kilometers from San Clemente, in the Tuyú
is the tomb of Santos Vega, where the orcas come in
and the surfers in their grass skirts, on the crystal waves
Broken crystal, ornery orcas of history: they go
to the harpooners with their hooks: they go
where the deck-clearings cleave: where, melted, the gaucho
takes out his jack-knife and disgraces himself:
it was history, that disgrace!
disgrace of lying in the Tuyú, of a widespread lying
The cannibals in that crystal harassed by rude waves;
and you, in that lethargy of rigor mortis, don't you take it
                          [lying down?
Take crystalline, plumed crests?

A unos kilómetros de San Clemente, en el Tuyú\está la tumba de Santos Vega, adonde acuden las toninas\y los surfistas en sus jabas, sobre las olas de cristal\Roto cristal, tercas toninas de la historia: van\donde los arponeros con sus garfios: van\donde los zafarranchos cachan: donde fundido el gaucho\saca el facón y se disgracia:\era la historia, esa disgracia!\disgracia de yacer en el Tuyú, de un yacer general\Los caníbales en ese cristal las rudas olas asaetan;\y tú, en esa pereza de la yertez, no jalas?\ Jalas de crestas cristalinas y empenachadas?

(degradée)

by Néstor Perlongher

tr. Molly Weigel

in mirrors you cross galleries with handmirrors
        galleries, glassy, of glass and slime, vista
of "virile" virtuosity, a glassiness of rounded cape,
        or "caped": so,
since if in that abyss, or alley—he pushes down—the neck
        of the girl—,
because if that fishneck, curved
        under that radiance, swims, mirror being born, jade and gl-
ass? takes it, and in that crossing, of the lamé
 radiance, I engrave: it cuts the circle, gives
        an "ending." and if the shining
stroll is used, green canvas signals
—for a green hanged man—, to go ahead, why not?
if that slipping, that hanging
        expanded?
and in the circle, of that fish-tail, a detail appears
        in "madder"? overtattooed decolleté, dredges
the breast; of the one who brands: cut glass,
        luminous, infected sliver, whose sticking-plaster, in the
alcohol of those gazes that gush, in the

Degradée by Nestor Perlongher (XUL #5 p.37)
recorres en espejo galerías con espejos de mano\galerías, vítreas, de vidrio y lama, ve\un
"viril" virtuosismo, una vidriosidad de escapulados,\o "pulados": pues,\porque si en ese
abismo, o callecita—baja—el pescuezo de la niña—,\porque si ese pezcuello,
doblegado\bajo ese resplandor, nade, espejo que nace, jade y vi-\drio? jala, y en ese recor-
rer, del resplandor\lamé, burilo; corta el ruedo, da\una "terminación". y si se usa\el deam-
bular brilioso señas de lona verde\—para un ahorcado verde—, verme, por qué no?\si ese
desliz, ese arrastrar se\amplía?\y en el ruedo, de ese pez-cola, aparece un detalle\en "purpu-
rina"? sobretatuado en el escote, draga\el seno; de ésa que hiere: vidrio cortado, tajo\lumi-
noso e infecto, cuyos esparadrapos, en el\alcohol de esas miradas que chorrean, en la

frigidity of that glaze, or simply the incense of that smoke
      penetrates
   the meat of the neck, marks the "alleys" of that
      gallows, as if that head, rolling, through starched,
   stiff petticoats, took it scorched. rhymed its
asperity of live furs, with that "brown" stole
      she
covered her shoulders with? —hiding that hairiness. and the
batrachian weakening, doesn't it lead
to the alligator's paws, stagnant, or arranged in a
certain inertia?...
                 but what scratches,
yes. penetrates, and won't keep quiet. not necessarily,
   [since already at the edge
      of those Sarmiento swimming pools, there's a mother
      drowning, and another stripping, on the palier, in front
         of some officials
it's that mother and that absence. the scene, framed in
         crystal, provides the radiance
of those paralytic spiders. That one, and maybe the other. because,
      in rolling, through those trembling passages, didn't she
suffer the discomfort of those stays, and the suffocation of those
   buttocks, the
weight of those tiaras, or pendants, or rings, already

frialdad de ese glacé, o nomás el incienso de ese humo\cala\la carne del pescuezo, marca los "caminillos" de esa\horca, como si esa cabeza, de rodar, por enaguas\almidonadas, tiesas, jale lo ase. rima su\ aspereza de pieles vivas, con esa estola de "marrón"\con que ella\se cubría los hombros? —disimulando esa pilosidad. y lo\batracio de ese desfallecer, no lleva\a las patitas de yacaré, estagnadas, o colocadas en una\cierta inercia?. . .\pero que lo que araña,\sí. cala, y no calla. no necesariamente, ya que al borde\de aquellas piletitas de sarmiento, hay una madre que\se ahoga, y otra que se desnuda, en el palier, delante\de unos oficiales\está esa madre y esa ausencia. el cuadro, enmarcado en\cristal, da el resplandor\de esas arañas paralíticas. Esa, y acaso la otra. porque\ella, al rodar, por esos pasillitos, azoga-dos, no\padecía el ahogo de esas ligas, y la sofocación de esos\panderos, el\pesar de esos brincos, o pendientes, o anillos, ya

excessive? and what's recharged, in that account, isn't it
an increase, the extravagance
of jewelled straps, or the anger
of a candle that hangs? perhaps
heaving with heat? of
which heaven is he speaking? oh panromances, oh
coral bunglings, oh
rhinestones in a rut of rhyming...

(degradée)

excesivos? y lo que se recarga, en esa cuenta, no\es la vuelta de más, el disparate\de enjoy-
ados breteles, o el enojo\de un cirio que pendea? deja\caer acaso el celo? de\qué cielo nos
habla? o paniamores, o\chafalonerías de coral, o\strasses como estros...\\(degradée)

Mme. Schoklender

by Néstor Perlongher

tr. Molly Weigel

Please see note on Perednik's "The Shock of the Lenders"

Decked out in prickly pears and gladioli: mother, how you whip
   those scenes
of candied bearcubs, those bitter honeys: how you flourish
the frothing featherduster: and the spiders: how
you scare the stunned brute with your acid strap: fasten, pound in, and
   crush:
crutches of a paraplegic mother: soiled pelvis, Turkish
   trousers: it's that mother who insinuates herself in the mirror offering
regalia of a night in Smyrna and baccarat: fasten and mark off: shed
the mother who offers herself changing into a befeathered lover,
   ruffle and ransacked: that plucking
of the mother who pulls down the gauzes of the whisky tumblers
   on the mouse
table: mother and runs: cuts off and hooking: and hiccups:
                                   hanging from
the mother's neck a bracelet of blood, pubic blood, of bullets
and bad guys: blood weighted by those bills and those creams we
ate too much of on the little table of light in the shadow of our
easy anniversaries: that giant tassel: if you took my balls as fruits of an

Mme. Schoklender by Néstor Perlongher
Ataviada de pencas, de gladiolos: cómo fustigas, madre, esas escenas\de oseznos acarame-
lados, esas mieles amargas: cómo blandes\el plumero de espuma: y las arañas: cómo\espan-
tas con tu ácido bretel el fijo bruto: fija, remacha y muele:\muletillas de madre parapléxica:
pelvis acochambrado, bombachones\de esmirna: es esa madre la que en el espejo se insinúa
ofreciendo\las galas de una noche de esmirna y bacarat: fija y demarca: muda\la madre que
se ofrece mudándose en amantes al plumereo, despiole y despilfarró: ese desplume\de la
madre que corre las gasas de los vasos de whisky en la mesa\ratona: madre y corre: cercena
y garabato: y gorgotea:\pende del\cuello de la madre una ajorca de sangre, sangre púbica,
de plomos\y pillastres: sangre pesada por esas facturas y esas cremas que\comimos de más
en la mesita de luz en la penumbra de nuestras\muelles bodas: ese borlazgo: si tomabas mis
bolas como frutas de un

intrepid and erect elixir: dingles from a glacé that sweetened you:
but killing you was going too far: sweetly: making myself eat
  from those
stiff small disgusts that crouch tender in the haughty castling of my
muscles, and that conch-er when you lick with your mother's mouth the
caverns of the rising, the waning: the caves:
                                        and I, did I penetrate you? I could
hardly stop myself like a drunk male of hinges, shapeless, withered from
tequilas, from putting myself up in syrup, penetrating your blondnesses
  of a mother offering themselves,
like an altar, to the son—minor and mannered? adopting your fan
wires, the jewels you carelessly drop chiming onto the table,
amid the tumblers of gin, indecorously greased with that archaic
rouge of your lips?
                        like a wanton wolf cub, I could, rise up,
behind your petticoats and lick your breasts, as you'd lick my nipples
and leave dribbling on my tits—which seemed to titillate—
the purr:
                of your murmuring saliva? the strap of your teeth?
could I mother?
                        like a gallant in ruins who surprises his sweetheart between

elixir enhiesto y denodado: pendorchos de un glacé que te endulzaba:\pero era demasiado
matarte: dulcemente: haciéndome comer de esos\ pelillos tiesos que tiernos se agazapan en
el enroque altivo de mis\muslos, y que se encaracolan cuando lames con tu boca de madre
las\cavernas del orto, del ocaso: las cuevas;\y yo, te penetraba? pude\acaso pararme como
un macho ebrio de goznes, de tequilas mustio,\informe, almibararme, penetrar tus
blonduras de madre que se ofrece,\como un altar, al hijo—menor y amanerado? adoptar tus
alambres de\abanico, tus joyas que al descuido dejabas tintinear sobre la mesa,\entre los
vasos de ginebra, indecorosamente pringados de ese rouge\arcaico de tus labias?\cual
lobezno lascivo, pude, alzarme,\tras tus enaguas, y lamer tus senos, como tú me lamías los
pezones\y dejabas babeante en las tetillas—que parecían titilar—el\ronroneo:\de tu saliva
rumorosa? el bretel de tus dientes?\pude madre?\como un galán en ruinas que sorprende a
su novia entre

the crude flies of the longshoremen, on the docks, when
in the buttons, spawns loose, his protected perfidy? that secret
pubic place? how therefore I clutched that hand-hold, those tapirs
encrusted with orchid crutches, velvetly suspicious;
and supporting with my same member the cankerous spume of your sex,
to unload on your forehead? You'd smile tassled between the drops of
     semen of
the longshoremen who on the dock took you from behind, mildly:
I snatched you: what did you imagine?

las toscas braguetas de los estibadores, en los muelles, cuando\laxa desova, en los botones, la perfidia a él guardada? ese lugar\secreto y púbico? cómo entonces tomé esa agarradera, esos tapires\incrustados como mangos de magnolia, aterciopeladamente sospechosos;\y sosteniendo con mi mismo miembro la espuma escancorosa de tu sexo,\descargar en tu testa? Sonreías borlada entre las gotas de semen de\los estibadores que en el muelle te tomaban de atrás y muellemente:\te agarré: qué creías?

79

by Nahuel Santana

tr. G. J. Racz

In '79, a surviving worker recalls:

He left work

                without knowing
                just where
                he was to enter

this "duty-free" shop of fear
that some see coming

                and squeeze inside themselves:

fist eye thought words...

                until they exist no more.

But others

                like him
                —no doubt—

grew up
with eyes
so wide open
that bullets passed through them without striking

                the retinas
                a writing pad

their memories:
the mother's dream

                a peephole

79 by Nahuel Santana (XUL #3 p.11)

En la /79, trabajador sobreviviente recuerda:\\Salió del trabajo\sin saber\por dónde\habría de entrar\a este "free shop" del miedo\que algunos ven llegar\y aprietan dentro suyo:\el puño el ojo el pensamiento, y las palabras. . . \hasta que ya no existen.\\Pero los más\como él\- sin dudas\\crecieron\con los ojos\tan abiertos\que las balas pasaron sin golpear\sus retinas\ fueron un cuadernario\los recuerdos:\el sueño de la madre\una mirilla

                              open
                              in the night

his wife waiting out

                              the pregnant moments
                              the children alone

lay down
for her sake
the memory

                    of her man returns still,
                    dust lingering over time;
                    stubbornly he comes back

lingers looks at us smiles

                              asks us
                              —and drawing nearer—
                              with us

for u
       (a
         n
         d
           o
             t
               h
                 e
                   r
                     s)
                       s
                    approaches the morrow.

12/7/79, 4:10 p.m.
Buenos Aires

abierta\por las noches\su mujer aguardaba\cada espera\los hijos, solamente,\reposaban\por
ella\aún regresa\la memoria del hombre\el polvo detenido sobre el tiempo;\porfiadamente
vuelve\se detiene nos mira se sonríe\nos pregunta\—y avanza—\con nosotros\por nos–\
(y)\-otros\acerca la mañana.
07/12/79 - 16,10 Hs.\Buenos Aires

H

by Nahuel Santana

tr. G.J. Racz

To sense( )it gone
                              in the foregoing
what was
                              the present( )
                              all said and done(?).

In (la/i)nternal
                              unity
(n/l)ight
                    within:
orifice crevice grotto
we traverse
                              without finding
—the end—.

The end—
                    at
presend
"The Goose that laid the golden eggs
by the
                         dawn's early light."
                         White-hot

H by Nahuel Santana
Sentir( )-lo ido\en lo previo\y el presente que( )\ha sido (?).\\En la unidad\(l'-
)interna\noche\adentro:\orificio grieta gruta\que recorremos\sin encontrar\- el fin—.\\
El fin-\-al\presente\"Gallina de los huevos de oro\que como\febo se asoma".\Candente

reality
on which no one wagers
knowing the outcome

        still we remain standing—:
"Ring around the rosy

        all fall down
so that Death

      may pass unseen."

Again one

        senses
        sits down

springs up
sets free

        and cannot

long for
or forget

        the reality
of what can be

        lived
from within,

        he was saying
            —without forgetting the fallen
        who are the best of all.

realidad\de la que nadie arriesga\sabiendo el resultado\aún seguimos estando—:\
"Suban las barreras\para que pase\la parca\y nadie vea".\\Uno vuelve\a sentirse\a sentarse\a
saltarse\a soltarse\y no puede\ni añorar\ni olvidar\la realidad\de lo que puede
ser\vivido\desde adentro,\decía\—sin olvidar los restos\que son sumos.

Miss Murkiness (fragments)

Emeterio Cerro

translated by K.A. Kopple

missMurkiness		swoops	was
who		the branch	betrothed
cutting thirst	Devil		was
pours	bites		Rome
rider			
who	Devil	screeching	
tonsured	space	mountain	gates
hand		frightens	round
uncurls		the plaza	marked
pollen	Devil		deflated
who			
buttons	grain		cried
knives		cinnamon	
row thorn		turkey	
ay!	Devil	tobacco	
tear	peak	afraid	fangs
archangel			furious
wounded			spurs
push soar		looks	southerners
ay	Devil	throws	
rosy	wave	craw	turkey
dagger	Devil		beloved

La barrosa (fragmentos)by Emeterio Cerro (XUL #3 p.37)
laBarrosa abate fue\quien la rama novia\hirientes sed Diablo fue\vierte muerde Roma\
cabalgante\quien Diablo gritona\tonsurada espacio montaña tranqueras\mano espantas
redondas\desrizan la plaza marcaron\polen Diablo mordida\quien\abotonadas granito
lloraba\cuchillas canela\boga espina el pavo\ay! Diabla tabaca\desgarra pico asustado
colmillos\arcángela furiosos\herida espuelas\puja vuelo mira sureñas\ay Diablo tira\
sonrosada onda buche el pavo\puñal Diablo amado

nibble	pricks			slips
of the		cinnamon	countrywomen	
Devil Hound		turkey	chickens	
ay!	the			crowds of indians
ay!		history		

mordisco punza resbala\del canela paisanas\Diablo Lebrel el pavo gallinas\ay! la indiada\ay! historia

"a crack . . ."
by Roberto Ferro

tr. Jorge Guitart

a crack
has split
the white desert
    defying
    its power
    linking
        every silence
    everywhere
        threatening
        to strangle
        every mark
        until it vanishes

a tenacious insistence
on the plains

only light
    goes along
        with such
        a dare

a thin column of soot
        fighting
        to the death

"una grieta..." by Roberto Ferro (XUL #3 p.14)
una grieta\ha cribillado\el desierto blanco\desafiando\su poder\que eslabona\los silencios\desde todos los confines\amenazando\estrangular\cada trazo\hasta ocultarlo\una tenaz porfía\en la llanura\sólo la luz\acompaña\tamaño\atrevimiento\\una delgada columna de hollín\batiéndose\a muerte

an army burnished with silence

only light
    will stop
    its being destroyed
    its death by crushing
        in the powerful mist

only the light
    echoing
      the challenge
        in your eyes.

con un ejército bruñido de silencio\sólo la luz\detendrá\su aniquilación\su muerte por aplas-
tamiento\en la bruma poderosa\sólo la luz\que en tus ojos\repite\el desafío.

"I think of a pine tree..."

by Roberto Ferro

tr. Jorge Guitart

I think
of a pine tree
of the shadow of an erect pine tree
of looking toward the shadow of an erect pine tree
and
I write
a shadow of a pine tree
I see
it is the shadow of a pine tree
              installed on the page by signs
I think
that a shadow is the inverse of light shining through
I read
a shadow of a pine tree
I think
              it is the shining reproduction
              of every pine tree
              in every eye
              dwelling upon every shadow.

"Pienso en un pino" by Roberto Ferro
Pienso\en un pino\en la sombra de un pino erguido\en la mirada hacia la sombra de un pino erguido\y\escribo\una sombra de un pino\veo\que es una sombra de un pino\instalada en la hoja por los signos\pienso que una sombra es lo inverso de la luz a través de\leo\una sombra de un pino\pienso\es la multiplicación iluminada\de todos los pinos\en todas las miradas\que se detienen en su sombra.

Eurydice Has Gone To The Agora
And Is Wearing A White Headdress
by Roberto Ferro

tr. Jorge Guitart

> That skull had a tongue in it and could sing once:
> how the knave jowls it to the ground, as if it
> were Cain's jaw-bone, that did the first murder!
>
> *Hamlet V, 1. Wm. Shakespeare*

CREON waits/the thin rinds of mimesis/they allege
                    walls
space with/illusion of a space b e y o n d
                                            the line always
here/mouth of a horizon (Im)pressed it will
personify it
                    by
                            the   incl
                                        ined   pl
                                                    ane/

indifferent
to discourse   to his hated (con)tent
CREON waits   on the wrong side of the opaque mirror
and his tragedy   is
                                ees
                                ot

Euridice Ha Ido Al Agora\Y Lleva Un Tocado Blanco En La Cabeza...
by Roberto Ferro (XUL #5 p.22)
CREONTE espera/las delgadas cáscaras murallas de mímesis/alegan el\ espacio con/su
ilusión de un espacio más a l l a ʌla línea siempre\aquí/boca de un horizonte (Im)preso
lo personif icará por\el pl\ano incli\nado/ʌal discurso indiferente CREONTE espera y su
tragedia\a su aborrecida (con)tienda en el revés del espejo opaco esɹǝʌ

Scene 1. (SA я EVIO, FULL LENGTH, NOT TOO TALL, MUST LOOK AROUND 45 YEARS OLD, FROWNING THEATRICALLY, WEARING A UNIFORM WITH HUGE SHOULDER PADS, SOUTH AMERICAN MILITARY STYLE, WITH LOTS OF MEDALS. THE BACK OF THE STAGE MUST LOOK LIKE BACKSTAGE.

NOTE TO THE SCRIPT WRITER: THE INSTRUCTIONS FOR THE ILLUSTRATOR MUST BE IN CAPITAL LETTERS AND IN PARENTHESES. IN DIALOGUES WRITE THE NAME OF THE CHARACTER SPEAKING.

```
The matter, as I see it, is very simple.
You are mis/taken regarding the proce-
dure. You are creating a problem. To hell
with it! (Bu)ry that guy Polineices. As
to the woman, that troublemaker, as well
as everybody else who is making a big
thing out of it, make them disappear.
That is your role. That should be your
final solution.
```

SA я EVIO

Sign: something that by nature or agreement evokes in the mind the idea of something else.

a slight cut in the skin of   the page
                    Xntigone

Cuadro 1,- (SAVERIO DE CUERPO ENTERO - NO MUY ALTO - DEBE APARENTAR UNOS 45 AÑOS - DE GESTO FRUNCIDO Y TEATRAL LLEVA UNIFORME CON GRANDES HOMBRERAS - AMPULOSO - A LA MANERA DE LOS MILITARES SUD\\AMERICANOS - MUCHAS MEDALLAS EL FONDO DEBE APARENTAR LA (TRAS)TIENDA DE UN ESCENARIO). NOTA PARA EL GUIONISTA: LAS INDICA-CIONES PARA EL DIBUJANTE DEBERAN SER EN MAYUSCULA Y ENTRE PARENTE-SIS. LOS DIALOGOS DEBERAN IR PRECEDI-DOS POR EL NOMBRE DEL PERSONAJE.
EL ASUNTO ES SIMPLE A MI MANERA DE VER, USTED\EQUI/BOCA EL PROCEDIMIENTO. PORQUE INVENTA SU PROBLEMA. ¡¡AL DEMONIO!! (EN)TIERRE A ESE POLICLINES. EN CUANTO A ESA ALBOROTADORA Y A TODOS CUANTOS ESTEN MOLESTANDO. (T) HAGALOS DESAPARECER ACHELOS DE SU PAPEL. ESA DEBE SER SU SOLUCION FINAL.   SAVEЯIO
S'igno. Cosa que por su naturaleza o convenio evoca en el/ entendimiento la idea de otra.
una escisión apenas en la piel de la hoja\Xntígona

42

with no ink tears   Xigone

an exorcism on the text gone Xigone

a slight deletion n one a singular

shift over the letters n in a sy

mmetrical plundering of letters so as not to see the Name

n XXne and only the distant trace

in the (h)

ole N N

repetition in the baptism of silence   N N

deletion by a dumb linguist who tours

the arsenal searching   b e   y   o   n   d

the mark

nn NN

zone

number returns

oNe by oNe in their turn

chosen

earth carries the visible $\left(\begin{array}{c}c \\ \text{rossed out}\end{array}\right)^{n}$

in the dead

leaving silence to the

per

ʌǝɹ   t

s S'

who will be emptied   now

sin ninguna lágrima de tinta nXígona\un exorcismo en el texto nXgona una leve supresión
n Xona un singular\desplazamiento sobre las letras n Xna un saqueo si\métrico para no ver
el Nombre\n nX y sólo la huella lejana\en el (hu) eco N N\la repetición en el bautismo del
silencio N N\una elipsis del lingüista que estúpido recorre el arsenal buscando más a l l a
'\de la marca\nn NN\zona\el número retorna\uNa a uNa a su turno es\cogidas\la tierra lleva
lo visible en\los muertos\(t achados)n\dejando el silencio a los p \e r\ɹǝʌ t i\d O' o\S' s\
que serán vaciados ahora

CREON: My fellow citizens, the Fates have straigthenfated out
the business of the city after having fatethrown it
into deep confusion

they will be emptifated
all r e v sions exhaustfated
now freed ■■■■■■ frombeing
sub
 ɹǝʌted
      by the blacksperm letters that
      were copulating with his eyes before
      the crucial and primitive cut
                        multiplicfated in the suture
it has been a spiralpinkveildiaphragmanticonceptual preterite
it has been washfated in the vaginas
of the pre(terit)text

$$\left(\begin{array}{c} (c) \\ \text{rossed out} \end{array} \right)^{n} \text{the in}$$
                  ɹǝʌsion
of the lingual coitus abortfated and curettagfated
it has XXXXXXX presence from their eyes

                              the struggle between word
                              and stroke
                              between stiletto and
                              eye

CREONTE; Ciudadanos, los Hados al fin han enderez/hado los asuntos de la ciudad
después de haberla agit/hado en revuelta confusión.\\que serán vaci/hados ellos ya
agot/hados de todas las versiones\ahora liber\deestar\sub\vertidos\por las letras de esperma
negra que\copulaban sus ojos antes del corte crucial y primigenio multiplic/hado en la sutu-
ra\ha sido un espiralvelorosadodiafragmanticonceptivo pretérito\se ha ase/hado en las vagi-
nas del texto (pre)\térito\((t)achado)n la in versión\del coito lingual abort/hado y rasp/hado
se ha XXXXXX de los ojos la presencia\\lucha de la palabra contra\el trazo\lucha del
estilete contra el\ojo

                                    that crashes
                              in the hol(low) silence
                                                of the stroke

the uNNameable has been erased from
the white throat   .
    possible now   the ear has been fateshut
the maze is almost tr ns
                        a   parent
the ground has been anointed by
the silencfated hinges of the
trace   there should no longer be
                                  any abstinence from the
                                  NName
CHORUS: What are you surmising now? That woman has disappeared
            before uttering a word, good or bad.

no ooz(th)ing deflowering will live on
in the infiltrafated (trans)vestites
white has been crownfated
                              by dint of cuts
that draw ■■■■■■ ossfated tibias
for the membranes of the text are now free
that some ripfated or crossfatedout
line of the tongue
that the recitals of the dampened evening have
                                        burn ished

que se estrella\en el silencio (hu)\eco de la marca\se ha borr/hado de la garganta blanca lo\
iNNombrable\ya es posible clausur/hado el oído\el laberinto es casi tr ns\a parente\la tierra
ha sido ungida por los\goznes silenci/hados de la\huella\ya no debe haber abstinencia del
NNombre\CORO: ¿Qué conjeturas ahora? Esa mujer ha desaparecido sin proferir buena ni
mala palabra.\ninguna defloración vis/cosa perdurará en los (tra)vestis in-filtra/hados se ha
coron/hado el blanco a fuerza de cortes que dibujan tibias cruz/XXXX que ya libres las
membranas del texto que alguna línea rasg/hada o anul/hada de la lengua que los recitales
\de la noche humedecida han\pul ido\en

45

CHORUS: But here is the king himself, carrying in his hands the evident signal not of someone else's blame but, if I may say so, of his own crime.

NNames NNnames and lists AND lists AND lists AND listas AND listslists
of those who do not exist in the (pro)
                              gram
of those who were not ƨqilled
there is no unity   a litany of nnames
once the Signifying is (c)rossed out there is no possible
                                        relation
                their/sub   bodies
                              tracted
                    ex
                              tracted their letters
they are nnothing   do not know phonocentrism
(nnames) of nonlooking residues
they now are re/boned
                    their bodies have been (ex)humed
but they will not be (ex)
                    pressed
shovelfuls of dirt(y words)
    n of (ec(h)o)log
CREON: What is it now?
MESSENGER: Your wife, Eurydice, is making inquiries in the agora
           about his son whom you have not namefated.

CORO: Pero he ahí al mismo rey, que viene llevando en las manos la señal evidente no de alguna culpa ajena, si me es permitido hablar así, sino de su propio crimen,\\NNombres NNombres y listas Ylistas Y listas Ylistas Y listas listaslistaslista\de los que no existen en el (pro)\grama\de los que no fueron\ɹǝʌtidos no hay unidad letanía de nnombres (t)achado el S'ignificante no hay relación\posible\sus cuerpos\traídos\de letra\no son nnada\ignoran el fonocentrismo\(nnombres) de los residuos sin la mirada\ellas ahora se re/huesan\sus cuerpos han\sido (ex)humados\pero ya no serán (ex)\presos\listas de pala(brota)s\n de los (hu)\ecos\CREONTE: ¿Qué hay ahora pues?\EL MENSAJERO: Tu mujer, Eurídice, pide en la ágora por su hijo a quien tú no has nombr/hado

Hipster's mask

Susana Chevasco

translated by K.A. Kopple

lineage of butterflies
  a bit perverse
  upon crucifying the statues
           one hears
   the giant's howls
     distant
  to the meetings of the men
what limitations to scheme
         masking
    this mysterious dementia
  of the beetles
in the desert's hygiene
       for example
   maintaining some concession
  trying to survive
 and all of it psychoanalytically correct

Antifaz de viva by Susana Chevasco (XUL #5 p.20)
linaje de mariposas\casi perverso\al crucificar las estatuas\se escucha\los aullidos del gigante\ajeno\a las tertulias de los hombres\qué limitaciones por ardid\enmascara\esta misteriosa demencia\de los escarabajos\en la higiene del desierto\por ejemplo\sostener alguna concesión\tratando de sobrevivir\y todo psicoanalíticamente correcto

Baby, you pose no more

Susana Chevasco

tr. K.A. Kopple

A salty death to the Menina malva rose
    dance the pavane assassin
  wide-eyed princess
     almost subdued
menina
      by sunlight I know
 owl palace swell
  the czar's oil fires
green sea
green velazquez
green green
      poppy and mommy
       watch
   the quiet menina watching
   cyclamen of canned cholera
   cardenals who love luxury
Torrential she is in the chair
     Execution!
     Execution!
(if she stirs from the painting)
     Execution!

Ya no poses más nena by Susana Chevasco
Menina malvarosa en sal muera\baila asesina pavana\la infanta mirona\casi
susurrada\menina\a sol sé\palacio de lechuza ola\los óleos incendios de zares\verde de
mar\verde velázquez\verde de verde\papi y mami\ miran\a menina quieta mira\ciclamen de
cólera en lata\cardenales que amén lujuria\torrencial está en la silla\¡ejecución!\¡ejecu-
ción!\(si sale del cuadro)\¡ejecución!

Shock of the Lenders

(Main Fragment)

by Jorge Santiago Perednik

tr. Molly Weigel

NOTE: The *Shock of the Lenders*, by Jorge Santiago Perednik, takes as its points of departure a 1981 murder case that became a national sensation in Argentina. The Shoklenders were an upper-middle class educated family displaying all the outward signs of success: the father, Mauricio, was an engineer; they lived in a fashionable Buenos Aires neighborhood; there were three children. On March 30th, 1981 a neighbor followed a thin trail of blood to the bodies of Mauricio and his wife Cristina in the trunk of the family car. The two sons, Sergio and Pablo, were missing. A country-wide search began, and in few days both sons were apprehended on horseback, one having fled to the north, the other to the south. The trial uncovered many skeletons in the family closet, including possible incestous relations between Cristina and both sons, and the involvement of Mauricio's engineering firm in international arms traffic. XUL #5 published a series of long poems dedicated to the subject. —MW

The most beautiful word of the language is stranger
Barbaric or Barbara
All men are mortal the shock lender is also
The most beautiful concept of the mother tongue
Sabotage?
We used to lend

El shock de los lender (fragmentos) by Jorge Santiago Perednik (XUL #5 p. 30)
La palabra más bella del idioma es extranjera\Bárbara o Barbara\ Todos los hombres son mortales también el shock lender es\El concepto más bello de la lengua\Sabotaje?*Prestá - bamos*

I tell you, not them
"Look for a new almost because the old one is dis   "

Cards thrown down simulating an Order
 Protean tense: the lapse
Preterite tense: the cosmos
  ultrapreterite: the lapse
       present: the preteriduction machine
  such brief moments xx'x x
Something's stopp

Beauty is the order of sabotage. No
The order of beauty is an effect of sabotage. No
Beauty is a...from the order of sabotaging the order of...No?

The day is too clear to see what's happening
: a link in the chain has been broke
: crystals colors solstice equinox have been broke
Too clear to see
The fear   what's hidden under   always
Hell? concentric circles Why not Paradise?
""Don't believe him it's all a   circumferences dis
setups of our police who I call dialing 666
and others call   oligice
                oligarchy
                oligophrenia

Se lo digo a Usted, no a ellos\"Búsquense una nueva casi porque la vieja se está des "\\Barajas que van saliendo y simulando un Orden\Tiempo protérico: el lapsus\Tiempo pretérito\el cosmos\ultrapretérito: el lapsus\ pre sente: la máquina pretéritoductora\ brevísimos\Algo se ha deteni\\La belleza es el orden de los sabotajes. No\El orden de la belleza es un efecto de los sabotajes. No\La belleza es un... de la orden de sabotear el orden de . . . ¿No?\\El día está demasiado claro para ver lo que sucede\: se ha rompido un eslabón de la cadena\: se han rompido los cristales los colores el solsticio el equinoccio\Demasiado claro para ver\ El miedo lo que se oculta bajo siempre\¿Infierno? círculos concéntricos ¿Por qué no Paraíso?\" "no le crea es todo circunferencias desc\trampas de nuestra policía que yo llamo discando el 666\y otros llaman oligocía\oligarquía\oligofrenia

oligoclase hematite mineraloligopoly(ce)
etc etc''''

decentered circumferences crossing such that
each point is the intersection of multiple discs such that
each point constitutes an existence   (note: you for example)

(nothingness—neeche— (the only—stirner—
bah—the story you tell is just too pat
in your guilt I smell a rat slither bite infect squeal
turn around, I'll make a note of that   turn around so he can steal you
or better: Truth is tails Beauty heads
both faces the being—duplicity—coin of this cosmos
the man who relates the eye and the finger
the name that relates flash and bang
what's more important, thunder or lightning?
Great balls of fire, I thought you'd never say it!

weapons, instruments of
The providers, etc
The commotion, etc etc
The corollaries that some call History
1. not to put up any more with the paternal hoop of the self or the law
2. to penetr (pay a price) assassin (shoot a) ate it
3. to be (nomen atque omen) the social lenders of the cause of
   maximum shock

oligistio hematites mineraloligopoli\etc etc''''\circunferencias descentradas atravesándose de
modo que\cada punto es la intersección de múltiples discos de modo que\cada punto con-
figura una existencia (apunto: verbigracia vos)\\(la nada -nische- (el único estirner\bah lo
que usted dice está mal dicho\en tu culpa hay un bicho galopa muerde contagia\date vuelta
que te ficho date vuelta que te plagia\o mejor: la Verdad es la ceca la Belleza el
escudo\ambas caras el ser la falsía la moneda de este cosmos\el hombre que asocia el ojo y
el dedo\el nombre que asocia fogonazo y estampido\ ¿cuál es más importante, el trueno o el
relámpago?\ ¡rayos, pensé que nunca lo dirías!\\armas, instrumentos de\Los prestatarios,
etc\La conmoción, etc etc\Los corolarios que algunos llaman Historia\1.- no soportar por
más tiempo la argolla paterna del ser o de la ley\ 2.- penetr(pagar un precio) asesin (pegar
un arla) \3.- ser (nomen atque omen) los lender sociales de la causa de máximo shock

51

Ego non baptizo te in nomine Diaboli et
Filii et Spiritus non Sancti—sed in nomine
Patris—madness is only definable negatively
amniotic fluid on the bodies
with her sister reason useless extremes one and the same rain from above
—not the (black) art of the deceivers but rather ascetic magic
Casing the city of god in the name of economy
Looking for special deals with Intelligence or Power or Angel
Bribing: Pull the trigger! Kill! (I'm waiting)

discovering a new kind of weapon: that has no one to aim at
                                        that has nothing to fire at
real weapons

CHORUS (intellectuals if possible)
The electrical charges called shocks
can be caused when the wires corrode
their mothers would like back their cocks
to get back some of what they are owed
Their crest illustrates as it mocks
two red lions attached to her nodes
as they try to get into her box

My good and merciful god, you know that I don't approve of this
That I don't approve of anything that offends you

Ego non baptizo in nomine Diaboli et\ Filii et spiritus non sancti—sed in nomine\ Patris—
la locura es definible solo negativa mentete\líquido anneótico sobre los cuerpos con su her-
mana razón extremos inútiles de una la misma lluvia de arriba\—no el arte (negro) de los
embaucadores sino ascética magia/En aras de economía recorrer la villa de dios/Buscar
tratos especiales con Inteligencia o Poder o Angel/Sobornar a ¡Gatillen!¡Maten! (los
espero)/descubrir armas de un nuevo tipo: que no haya a quien apuntar/que no haya que
disparar/verdaderas armas\\CORO (en lo posible intelectuales)\En otros tiempos llama-
ban\a los shock eles chocones\por venir esos varones\de mujeres que deseaban\que les rin-
dan sus cojones\Los emblemas lo ilustraban\ dos rubicundos leones\prendidos de los
pezones\de una madre que horadaban\\Mi buen y misericordioso dios, tú sabes que yo no
apruebo esto\ Que no apruebo nada que te ofenda

Yet you will approve it: habit and greed
But lord, the heart of an upright man...I mean, the abominations . . .
  Leviticus VIII
Better sleep and dream

And the dream was: a sort of viaduct in the mountain
The watch casting its hands like arrows or syringes against the eyes
A horse with two blind heads quartering the body
And the dream was:
A horse with six feet two heads escaping one to the north the other to
  the south
Vanished. It was:
I was drawing trying to capture the landscape: that tree populated with
  birds against the horizon
Before (or first and not before) something had captured me: many birds
  no horizon
and the riders moving away one to the great salt marsh the other to the
  glacier on the same animal
Vanished. It was:
I was running with the spear which was a pencil in my hand after the bird
  with white wings. Two wings
The order was to capture the bird draw it bring it back transformed into
  a hero
The horse told me our hero will be two, and with us, three, the great hero,
  the excluded
Vani   It wa li an instant

Ya lo aprobarás: costumbre y avaricia\Pero señor, el corazón de un hombre recto. . . quiero
decir, las abominaciones... Levítico VIII...\ Mejor duérmete y sueña\\Y la sueña fue: una
especie de viaducto en la montaña\Y el sueño fue:\Un caballo con seis patas dos cabezas
escapando una rumbo al norte otra rumbo al sur\Se desvaneció. Fue:\Yo dibujaba para atra-
par el paisaje: ese árbol poblado de pájaros contra el horizonte\Antes (o primero y no antes)
algo me había atrapado: muchos pájaros ningún horizonte\y los jinetes alejándose rumbo a
la gran salina rumbo al ventisquero en un mismo animal\Se desvaneció. Fue:\Yo corría con
la lanza que era un lápiz en la mano tras el pájaro de alas blancas. Dos alas\la orden era
capturar al ave dibujarla traerla convertida en héroe\ El caballo me dijo nuestro héroe serán
dos, y con nosotros, tres, el gran héroe, el excluido\ Se desv Fu com   un soplo

Che Guevara is mixed up in this story Mickey Mouse is mi
Do you believe in Christ? Yes. And in Longfellow?
The shot of the blowgun. Again. The death blow.
The best allies of the Fathers are the Dead
Deadfellow: "the Man with the Great Beard has sent me up here to
to test the effects of that is you know"

A man / ElseWhere?
Can / A man A man / Make / Social Revolution?
Can / A man / Make / Social Revolution / ElseWhere ElseWhere?

hero he who has won a battle and lost his   and because of that is a hero

The Topos Uranus, the King of Heaven, the Socialrevolutzie: the Future
    the OtherPlace
The best allies of the Fathers are
weapons, instruments of
the owners of the sacred house
General Investment Company The Beyond. Everything goes better with
    faith in Us.

"the Venture is the Adventure" they repeated "the Venture is the
    Adventure" for thirty-eight minutes children laughing like crazy
And if the children were ri

El Che Guevara se ha metido en esta historia el Ratón Mickey se ha me\¿Usted cree en Cristo? Sí. ¿Y en Longfellow?\El tiro de cervatana. Otra vez. El tiro de gracia\Los mejores aliados de los Padres son los Muertos\Deadfellow: "el Hombre de la Gran Barba me ha enviado a estas alturas a \a probar los efectos de en fin usted sabe"\\¿UN hombre/Otra Parte?\¿Puede/UN hombre UN hombre/Hacer/La Revolución Social?\¿Puede/UN hombre/Hacer/La Revolución Social/En Otra Parte En Otra Parte?\\héroe el que ha ganado una batalla y ha perdido la y por ello es héroe\\El Topos Uranos, el Reino de los Cielos, la Socialrevolutzie: el PorVenir el OtroLugar\Los mejores aliados de los Padres son\ armas, instrumentos de\ los dueños de la sagrada casa\Compañía General de Inversiones El Más Allá. Todo va mejor con fe en Nosotros\\"la Ventura es la Aventura" repitieron "la Ventura es la Aventura" durante treinta y ocho minutos los niños a las carcajadas\¿Y si los niños tuvieran raz

"Shut up!" Signed: Destiny (S Freud Stars Religion Science Hitler
                       V. I. L. Buenito Mussolini the Race the Party the
                       Corporation ersatz hybrids etc don't take another
                       step against against the)
                       Destiny
                             In God We Trust
Oremus:
Blessèd Abstraction Almighty Abstraction may you sustain our lives and
   give them a purpose
the Mystery the House of Mist: (the other—or Go)Destiny
Tiny reason that establishes order
"It's natural for the many to submit to the few" could be used as a
   subordinate
              "for the many to submit to the only" it could be said that
"It's natural to use subordinates"
What many, Few and Only like, Order
That which identifies Everyone

"The Venture is the Adventure" they repeated "the Venture is the
   Adventure"
"Shut up!"

because. the desert. this ineffectual conspiracy of circumstances

Disguised as a boy who plays the flute

";¡A callar!" Firmado: el Destino (S Freud los Astros la Religión la Ciencia Hitler V.I.L.
Buenito Mussolini la Raza el Partido la Corporación híbridos sucedáneos etc no de un paso
más en contra de\de los) el Destino\In God We Trust\Oremus:\Bendita Abstracción Ilustre
Abstracción que sostienes nuestras vidas y les das un propósito\el Misterio la Casa de la
Niebla: el D(ios—o el otro—) Es Tino\"Es natural que los muchos se sometan a los pocos"
pudiéndose utilizar como subordinada\"que los muchos se sometan al Unico"\El Tino que
establece el orden\pudiendose decir que\ "Es natural usar subordinadas\ Lo que a muchos,
Pocos y Unico les gusta, el orden\ Aquello que identifica a todos\"La Ventura es la
Aventura" repitieron "la Ventura es la Aventura"\"¡A callar!"\\porque. el desierto. esta
ineficaz confabulación de circunstancias\\con el disfraz de un muchacho que toca la flauta

He asked if death were unitary or real
And she said: little is know about bodies, about matter
Behind a door there's another door and
Behind that door there's another door and
Behind
       one more door and
Behind
       there's

Obsessions

CHORUS (if possible, id., id.)
They gave their father forty licks
then took a scissors to his dick
those boys are full of dirty tricks
and this is how they get their kicks
If it's not broken, what's to fix?
They climbed up on their mama's back
and rode her all around the track
they said, we'll give you what you lack
our darling nymphomaniac
Their morals are a little slack
but they make up for it in tact
they may be just a pair of pricks
but they're our boys through thin and thick

Preguntó si la muerta era unitaria o real\Y ella dijo: Poco se sabe de los cuerpos, de la materia\Detrás de una puerta hay otra puerta y\Detrás de esa puerta hay otra puerta y\Detrás\una otra puerta hay otra puerta y\Detrás\hay\Obsesiones\CORO\(en lo posible id., id.) Ultimamente llamaban\a los chocones shock eles\por ser un par de peleles\que a todos conmocionaban\A papá ahíto atacaban\a mamá rito violaban\de papá el pito cortaban\de mamá el mito mataban\¡caramba que eran muy crueles!\ Santana entre los Ranqueles\Edipo en los anaqueles\los curas para sus fieles\los poetas en los burdeles\sin dudar lo pregonaban\ ¡los héroes son los shock eles!

Stupidity and Truth—what does this prove?
In the archetype someone empties himself, says
The duty of killing them (*solvere*)
Cutting the damned knot and solving the problem
That is not vanity

(Later, at the wake, the family will change the story
(They won't dissolve the raveled thread of a decayed knot into nothing
They won't say "the debts will be discharged. So it has been written."
"Someday you'll repay (resolve) everything I've done for you")
They'll tell it oh literature as the payment of a debt)

Not even to tell something at most a little something to say for example
poetry is not truth
             not beauty
                     leaves someone burns against the cold

The adventure will be poetically: a writing that says:
the pick parted both sides of the cranium entered the secret vagina and
   reason shuddered
the ence*phallic* tissue crossed the broken membrane showed the world its
   horrors and reason was freex
and that man who had raised a family amounted to something in life
made great sacrifices for his children provided an education

Estupidez y Verdad ¿qué prueba esto?\En el arquetipo alguien se vacía y dice\El deber de matarlos (*solvere*)\Cortar el nudo maldito y resolver el problema\Eso no es vanidad\(En el velorio, más tarde, los deudos cambiarán la historia\(No disolverán en la nada la hilacha de un nudo podrido\No dirán la deudas serán cumplidas. Es lo que ha sido escrito"\("Alguna vez pagarás (resolverás) todo lo que hice por vos")\La contarán oh literatura como el pago de una deuda)\contar ni siquiera algo a lo sumo alguito decir por ejemplo/la poesía no es la verdad\no es la belleza\unas hojas que alguien quema contra el frío\La aventura poéticamente será: un escrito que dice:\el pico *separó* ambos lados del cráneo entró en la vagina secreta y la razón se estremeció\la masa ence*fálica* cruzó la membrana rompida asomó sus horrores al mundo y la razón se liberó\y ese hombre que había formado una familia llegado a ser alguien en la vida\hecho grandes sacrificios por sus hijos dado una educación

even read Schiller in the original and Hegel's Logic
only managed to say "Sometimes you forget that you are my son"

The big raw chunks must be eliminated it must be served well done
"today in school we baked cookies" says the oldest, five years old. His
brother, three, replies, "and we had them half-baked"
laughter in the room. Coughs

"I've given you everything and I am nothing."
"Now I receive your gifts, which I do not deserve."

the end of the adventure will be:
the horse that falls down and "he makes trouble like this" say the children
    kicking their legs
"you ran him too hard" the keeper accuses them "you profited too much"
    pronounce the bankers of Amberes
"you've gone" sentences the executioner "too far"

a vehicle for crossing the deed of America *I will ride my father for eight
    thousand kilometers*
an animal with a black forehead who makes trouble with his feet *If he's
    no use he's got to be put down*
the burro the messiah will use to reach Jerusalem *He frightens me he
    bites he has a big wee-wee*
the rolls royce of the magnates? *If He's No Use He's Got to Be Put Down*

incluso leído a Schiller en su idioma original y la Lógica de Hegel\ sólo atinó a decir "A
veces vos te olvidás que sos mi hijo"\\Hay que eliminar los fragmentos de gran crudeza hay
que darlo todo cocinado\"hoy me dieron en la escuela mate cocido" dice el mayor, de cinco
años. Contesta\el hermano, tres años, "y a mí mate cocido con aguja e hilo" risitas en la
sala. Toses\\"Les he dado todo y soy nada."\"Ahora recibo vuestros dones, que no merez-
co"\\el fin de la aventura será:\el caballo que cae al piso y "arma jaleo así" dicen los niños
agitando las piernas\"lo corrieron demasiado" les recrimina el guardián "lucraron demasia-
do" diagnostican los banqueros de Amberes "han ido" sentencia el verdugo "demasiado
lejos"\\un vehículo para cruzar la hazaña de América *montaré a mi padre por ocho mil
kilómetros*\un animal que tiene la frente negra y arma jaleo con las patas *si no sirve hay que
matarlo*\el burro que usará el mesías para subir a Jerusalem *me da miedo muerde tiene la
cosita de hacer pipí muy grande*\¿el rol rois de los magnates? *Si No Sirve Hay Que Matarlo*

Because they can't connect the beginning with the end, observed
   subinspector Alcmeon,
the shocklenders die
that's why so many die—so many—and we don't understand why.
Nothing connects with nothing.

The end of the adventure will be: the adventure doesn't end
It's the fourth psychic instance, it's the mystery
decentered circumferences crossing such that
"Sometimes you forget that I am your son"
Machines that make the past present such that
"Very few, unfortunately"

The adventure will be poetically: a writing that says: Too clear to see
The opening Two points
Where the father has been there the son is resurrected
The two cords the knot cut   *is printed*
                         "no, don't print it!" "Forget!"
His cloudied storied

Porque no pueden unir el principio con el fin, observó el Subinspector Alcmeón,\los shock
lender mueren\por eso es que tantos mueren (tantos y tantos) y no comprendemos
porqué.\Nada se une con nada.\\El fin de la aventura será: la aventura no tiene fin\Es la
cuarta instancia psíquica, es el misterio\circunferencias descentradas atravesándose de
modo que\"A veces usted olvida que soy su hijo"\Máquinas para hacer presente el pasado
de modo que\"Muy pocas y lo lamento"\\La aventura poéticamente será: un escrito que
dice: Demasiado claro para ver\La abertura Dos puntos\Donde el padre ha pasado allí el
hijo resuscita\Las dos cuerdas el nudo corte *se imprime*\ "¡no, no lo impriman!"
"olvidea!"Su turbía historía

Sophia (excerpt)

by Luis Thonis

tr. G. J. Racz

If the prior condition does not occur in the premise
if the postponed culmen does not occur in a destructive dilemma
in three shakes of a tentacle
 if hyperbole does not display a halcyon in passing

                                —'isous—

unreal subjunctivity acquires more restraint still
in the enhancing delay of its hysteron proteron

                             a delicate moment indeed

Sophia

       if A and B are contemporaries of B
       it does not follow that P must be a contemporary of B
       which fails to connect the pasts
       in the enhancing delay of its hysteron proteron

Sophia

       quisque miseracordia abes

                         carissima

          you are probably aware that quisque means quisqumque
          an ever so slight transmutation of subject,

I spoke of damsels, not of women
 hysteria was not the only way of looking young
to initiate with furrowed brow a visit to the islands
was not something which in its lassitude had obligation for a parallel
like adapting cardinally to a new world

"Sophia (fragmentos)" by Luis Thonis (XUL #5 p.46)
Si la condición previa no acaece en la premisa\si el postergado culmen no se da en dilema destructivo\en los tres movimientos tentaculares\si la hipérbole no acusa un alción al paso\—'isous—\la subjuntividad irreal adquiere otra mesura\en la espera potenciada de su hýteron próteron\un momento de delicadeza\Sophia\si A y B son contemporáneos de B\no se sigue que P haya de ser contemporáneo de B\lo que desacierta los pasados\en la espera potenciada de su hýteron próteron\Sophia\quisque misericordia abes\carissima\sabrás que quisque vale por quisqumque\levísima transmutación de un sujeto\hablé de doncellas no de mujeres\si la histeria no ha sido el único modo de parecer joven\incoar a ir a las islas con el ceño restringido\no era algo que en su lasitud tuviera la obligación por paralelo\como el adaptarse cardinal a un nuevo mundo

for the mere fact of having been born
yea, Sophia
                    says Anna Livia
                              the Irish whore
  de te fabula narratur
              eco admisso
                    Hippolyta would not have heard
                                        that depraved proleptic
we live in an age of wonders!   Proserpina
it might have been necessary
              to initiate
                    initiare
the placenta of Rousseau, Customs Officer,
              a dance of multicurled tones
that took the capers of fish drowning between rosy fingers
as haruspices for the uniform space of underground minimachias
        and thus took epiteths and epitomes from birth
with uproarious laughter
  per Chaos hoc ingens silentia regni
    a thousand orders irreducible to one lone genesis
    a specific type of order prevails in each era
    in the shelter of an emphatic archipelago spreading out among fibrils
hyperbole
              is suitable for use until the age of twenty-five

por el solo hecho de haber nacido\yeá Sophia\dice Anna Livia\la puta irlandesa\de te fabula
narratur\eco admisso\que no oyera Hipólita\la prava proléptica\we live in age of won-
ders!\Proserpina\necesario hubiese sido\el incoar\el inchoare\la placenta del aduanero
Rousseau\danza de los tonos polirrizos\que tomaba como arúspices para el espacio uni-
forme de las minimaquias subterráneas\los cabrilleos de los peces que se anegan entre los
dedos rosados\tomaba así los epítetos y los epítomes natales\con amplísima risa\per Chaos
hoc ingens silentia regni\mil órdenes irreductibles a una sola génesis\en cada época domina
un tipo específico de orden\al socaire de un archipiélago enfático que se reparte entre fibril-
las\la hiperbolé\conviene usarla hasta los veinticinco años

the Stagirite advised
Anatomy of Melancholy
that Apollonius of Tyana enters a temple to subvert the idols
Apollonius the unmasker
this was in the days of the Sage when the gust sufficed
Sophia
listen to Erasmus hanging from the canopy of heaven
someone elucidating a sky without a haruspex
quod erat demostrandum at the foot of the phosphorescent enthymeme
eco admisso
taking away a sun
from the Civitas Solis
I spoke of damsels
Campanella's laughter in the meadowlark dawn
the meadowlark forgot the swallow
as the moon ceased to reflect Hamlet
earth and death
are very close to man here
what happens when earth and death unite

aconsejó el Estagirita\Anatomy of Melancholy\el de Tiana, Apolonio, entra a un templo para desbaratar los ídolos\Apolonio el desenmascarador\eran los tiempos del Sabio y bastaba el soplo\Sophia\escucha a Erasmo colgado de la bóveda celeste\alguno dilucidando un cielo sin arúspice\quod erat demostrandum al pie del entimema fosforescente\eco admisso\quitando un sol\de la Civitas Solis\hablé de doncellas\la risa de Campanella en la alborada de una alondra\la alondra olvidó la golondrina\como la luna dejó de reflejar a Hamlet\la tierra y la muerte\aquí están muy próximas a los hombres\qué pasa cuando se aúnan la tierra y la muerte

Pedestrian

by Gustavo Röessler

tr. G.J. Racz

```
                              T
                              H
L                             E          has
    imagined                             LOST
I                             S
                      lie     T          i
B    s   W      t             A          t
                              I          s
E    u   H      u             R          s
                    and       W          s
R    n   E      b             A          t
                              Y          e
T    s   R      e                        p
                              of         s
Y    e   E      d
                              R
     t   cold   u             E
         moons  p             A
                              S
                              O
                              N
```

PEATONAL by Gustavo Röessler (XUL #5 p.41)
LA\LIBERTAD\ocaso\imaginado\DONDE\frías lunas\yacen\entubadas\y\LA ESCALERA\
de la\RAZON\ha\PERDIDO\sus peldaños

Still Life
by Gustavo Röessler

tr. G. J. Racz

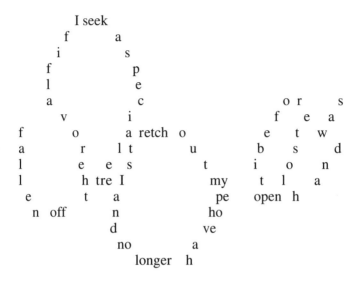

```
            I seek
         f        a
       i           s
      f              p
      l               e
      a                c              o   r       s
        v            i               f   e   a
f         o       a retch o             e   t   w
a         r      l t         u         b   s       d
l         e  e  s             t        i   o       n
l         h tre I                my    t   l       a
 e        t    a                pe    open h
   n  off      n                ho
               d                ve
            no         a
          longer    h
```

NATURALEZA MUERTA by Gustavo Röessler
caído del árbol si busco un sabor especial\y estiro mi mano abierta\ y ya no espero\antes que se haya perdido

"Secret. . ."

by Arturo Carrera

tr. K. A. Kopple

secret
ultimately secret. Father
who calls
and who talks to the cat
his aching call
so silent he and he but
a happy yawn
and they talk to the cat
the yawn
without him,

On the vatek terrace: I know
he was in Vátek:
filthily immersed in
his solitude and happy yes
happy, more faithful in his
longing. Drowned, drowned from
tedium........................
.... yes

"Secreto. . ." by Arturo Carrera #5 p.7
secreto\últimamente secreto, Padre\que llama\y que discute con el gato\su llamado
doloroso\tan silencioso él y él como\el bostezo feliz\y que discuten con el gato:\sin él,\\En la
terraza vatek; yo sé\que estaba en vátek\suciamente volcado a\su soledad, y el felis sí\feliz,
más fiel en sus an-\helos. Ahogos, ahogos del\tedio...........\...............sí

The father

by Arturo Carrera

tr. K. A. Kopple

The father,

Given that he vibrates in the printed, codified helicoidal ribbon: given
that he permits and "silences" the coloring book of some celibate and
scratched little faces, little tails. Given that he has flung himself at
Woman the night inundates him, the night pampers him and baths him
and heralds him: now free of his sex in his History-Volume, his facts, his
hagiographies permanently decked out in gold: his vacilating sensations
of remote acids and chances where a Thunder-Father and another
Trembling anxiously welcome the unformed droplet: father who sepa-
rates himself from his scrotal book: father who abadons the pimply plea-
sure of his assessed goldbrick. Sucked up spiral of quieted paternity: I'll
make a locus solus out of you. Your palpitating javeline forgotten by her
in him. And he of your book eternal in illusion. All of the imaginary wave
of suffering: reading? Father what? With this stuttering gunfire of images
steadily emptying lead and gold into me.

The father gen, erative
of desire.

El padre by Arturo Carrera (XUL #5 p.7)
El padre, \\Dado que vibra, en la cintilla helicoidal impresa, codificada: dado que admite y
"calla" el simulcop de unas caritas, colitas célibes y rayadas. Dado que arrojado en la
Mujer la noche lo inunda, la noche lo contiene y lo empapa y lo enuncia: libre del sexo ya
en su Tomo-Historia, sus datos, sus hagiografías tercas en la engayadura dorada: sus vaci-
lantes sensaciones de ácidos remotos y azares donde un Padre-tronador y otro Tembloroso
admitían con ansiedad la gotita informada: padre que se separa de su libro escrotal: padre
que se abandona en el acmé del goce su lingote asesor. Aspirada espiral de paternidad
callada: un *locus solus* hará de ti. Tu jabalina palpitante la olvidó ella en él. Y él de su
libro entero en ilusión. Toda la soñada onda del doleer: leer? Papá qué? Con ese tableteo
tartamudo de la imágenes asegurándose en plomo y oro en mí. \\ El padre gen, erial del
deseo.

"I observe the smallest..."

by Arturo Carrera

tr. K.A. Kopple

I observe the smallest
the most simple, the most insignificant.
my modus operandi regarding the children
should be modified.
nothing develops more harmoniously
to a child
than having a plan in spite of everyone

recently
I was baptised by what I needed,
a baptism for the new comer different from
a baptism not by aspersion;
I was submerged in the water with my eyes
shut
but return to the surface,
ascending to the temptation of another tiny distant place

... having a plan in spite of everyone: that is poetry...
... having a plan, a map of self-confidence, a hope encoded where paternity is pulverized, where the golden rib and an ash body cry out for the uncertain night. . . . .

"yo observo lo más pequeño..." by Arturo Carrera (XUL #7 p.7)
yo observo lo más pequeño\lo más simple, lo más insignificante\mi plan de operaciones respecto de los niños\deber ser modificado.\no hay nada que desarrolle más armoniosamente\a un niño\que mantener un plan a pesar de todos\\\en estos últimos tiempos\recibí un bautismo del que tenía necesidad,\un bautismo para el recienvenido en lo que separa\un bautismo no por apersión;\yo estaba sumergido en las aguas con los ojos\cerrados\pero vuelvo a la superficie,\asciendo a la tentación de otra pequeña lejanía\\...mantener un plan a pesar de todos: es la poesía...\...mantener un plan, un mapa de la confianza en sí\mismo, una esperanza cifrada donda la paternidad se\pulveriza: donde reclama para la noche insegura una\costilla de oro y un cuerpo de cenizas.....................

Patrimonies 1981

by Susana Cerdá

tr. Molly Weigel and Ernesto Livon Grosman

I
And after: this war
we return
to be goddesses
or perhaps gods.
—I ask myself without any
question mark
responding
without any
answer mark—

After: (the past provoked by the verb, linked with the preposition:
   the only plural position that ends in preparing the place.
   Place of delight where one persistently searches for: EXIT.
   Eruption, disruption, a tear, evacuation.
   We have. We are being, have been thrown toward another.
   Place.)

After: this which so much resembles coitus, or its successful
progression, over there, after bawling and whining in front of all the
schools, the ineffectual body stretched: to the North, to the South (or

Patrimonios 1981 by Susana Cerdá (XUL #7 p.10)

I\Y después de: esa guerra\volvemos\a ser diosas\o quizás dioses.\ -Me pregunto sin ningún signo\de pregunta\respondo\sin ningún\ signo de respuesta-\\Después de: (el pasado incitado por el verbo, en comunión con la preposición:\única plural posición que concluye en armar el sitio.\Sitio de un regodeo adonde se insiste en: la salida.\ Erupción, irrupción, lágrima, deposición...\Hemos. Henos siendo, sido lanzados hacia otro. Lugar.)\\
Después de: eso que tanto se parecía al acto, o a su recompensada progresión, ahí, luego de berrear, de patalear ante todas las escuelas, el fallido cuerpo se alargó: hacia el Norte, hacia el Sur (o

to the sides), in deserving formulas that whip indexes...

Swelling banner: the wind of each day.
Days off or days of excitement.
Corpulent, sweating words fluttering down, oh! this fall and others
        and others.
A fall that never stopped
falling
suspended dissolution
semen that before scattering
already was: Victory!

II
Between Victory and Defeat, categories proliferated, through
        which One
roved at ease, shouting for her: Freedom.
Echoes of the grapeshot aiming at them. The enemy.
"Damned sons of bitches"—
And then, this: the War.
Falling like the law of gravity.
All that, was accelerated its fall, to the rhythm of the fighting, under
        this sovereign law.
Speed that devastated the mirrors of the mirrors.

"...the art of invisibility."
Bye bye.
Goodbyes.

hacia los costados), en formulas merecedoras que latigueaban índices...\\Ondulante ban-
dera: viento de cada día.\Días de recreo o de agitación.\Corpulentas, sudorosas palabras
panfleteando, ay!, esa caída y otras y otras.\Caída que no terminaba\de caer\suspendida dis-
olución\semen que antes de derramarse\ya era: Victoria!\
II\Entre la Victoria y la Derrota, proliferaban las categorías, por las que Uno\ambulaba, a
sus anchas, gritando por ella: la Libertad.\Ecos de las metrallas apuntando a aquél. El ene-
migo.\ "Malditos hijos de perra."-\Y entonces, aquella: la Guerra.\ Cayendo como la ley de
gravedad.\Cuanto era, aceleraba su caer, al ritmo del guerrear, bajo esa soberana
ley.\Velocidad que arrasó con los espejos de los espejos.\\"... el arte de la invisibilidad."\
Aden. Aden.\Adioses.

III

As soon as the waters seemed calm
after this:
I surveyed what remained;
leaning out, I saw: my own gaze.
A gaze that saw. A form rippling.
I felt the undulation of my hips
following the beat.
Has the breeze
been stirring up the puddle?

IV

Now: the smoke, its grayish maneuverings:
in a ring, in triangles,
in forms of dispersing display.
An Eye notices the frequency of the shadings,
the string of gestures
—musical time captured—
deplores the margin
initiates the fragments.
Rhythmic.
Now: who could brag about love!

III\En cuanto parecieron estacionarse las aguas\después de:\mire lo que quedaba en
ellas,\asomada ví: mi mirada.\Mirada que vio. Una figura oscilaba.\Sentí el ondularse de
mis caderas\irguiendo un compás.\Habrá sido la brisa\agitando el charco?\

IV\Ahora: el humo, sus grisáseos conciliábulos:\en ronda, en triángulos\en formas de des-
perdigada exposición.\Un Ojo advierte la frecuencia de los matices,\el engarce de los
gestos\recorta espacios\compás capturando\deplora un margen\inicia los
fragmentos.\Acompasados.\Ya: quién podría jactarse del amor!

V

The gravity of the law of gravity
presses in
places me in certain corners
curls at my feet
living on
at the feet of the goddesses
surviving
at your feet.
In the Beyond.

VI

If it is by mathematics, for mathematics, from a mathematics, that:
      I love you.
If it is by love, for a love, from a love, that: mathematics.
Because other laws follow certain steps, certain days.
Shadows flashing the singular.
Cosmetics of a contradance.
Against what?
Sophisticated tastes
walling themselves up
in Chinese boxes.

Fortress of language?

V\La gravedad de la ley de gravedad\pesa\me deposita en ciertos rincones\se acurruca a mis pies\vivientes sobre\a los pies de las Diosas\sobrevivientes\a tus pies.\Más allá.\

VI\Si es por la matemática, para la matemática, desde una matemática que: te quiero.\Si es por el querer, para un querer, desde un querer, que: la matemática.\Porque otras leyes siguen algunos pasos, algunos días.\Sombras fulgurando lo singular.\Cosmética de una contradanza.\Contra qué?\Sofisticados sabores\amurallándose\ en las cajas chinas.\\Fortaleza del lenguaje?

Orient that doesn't know: to say no.
Orient that doesn't know: to say yes.
Orient that doesn't know?

O, really?

VII
From the most distant temples
where the only prayer spoken is your name.
I have returned.
To play "Survivor and Corpse."
I have come.
To the foot of renunciation,
in the vulgar mouth
thanks to the body
for the shout.
To the letter: I put the period.
I pass it, I unravel the lines
I move the borders.
I pat my hair
I take it in my fingers
distracted,
with the left hand or with
the right hand
I let it fall.

Oriente que no sabe: decir que no.\Oriente que no sabe: decir que sí.\Oriente que no sabe?\\Oh, riente!\

VII\Desde los mas lejanos templos\donde sólo se reza: tu nombre.\He vuelto.\A jugar a los vivos y a los muertos.\He venido.\Al pie de la renuncia,\en boca de lo cursi\gracias al cuerpito\por el grito.\Al pie de la letra: pongo el punto.\Lo paso, destejo las líneas\muevo las fronteras.\Tanteo mis cabellos\los tomo entre los dedos\distraída,\con la mano izquierda o con\la mano derecha\ los dejo caer.

Not so distracted.
I have come to laugh at what I don't understand.
I make: "APPLAUSE."
Combat of the hips.
I open my beautiful legs. Beautiful.
He remains absorbed in love.
I kneel to bless his swollen sex. Swollen.
I interrupt the invocation.

VIII
Just to enjoy being:
a woman.
With this fist still bleeding from its crime.
I will make of your joy, this: Semantic Liquid.
Neither defeated nor victorious:
Surrendered.
With expressions of admiration
as the gods like.

IX
If something of this effect
contracts patrimony
if the sayings
are said
and by the way

No tan distraída.\He venido a reírme de lo que no entiendo.\Hago: La "claque".\Combate de caderas.\Abro mis hermosas piernas. Hermosas.\Permanece absorto en el amor.\Me arrodillo a bendecir su sexo henchido. Henchido.\Interrumpo la invocación.\

VIII\Por el solo gusto de ser:\una mujer.\Con este puño que aun sangra de su crimen,\haré de tu goce, ese: Semántico Liquido.\Ni derrotados, ni triunfantes:\Rendidos.\Con signos de admiración\ como quieren los dioses.\

IX\Si algo de este efecto\contrae patrimonios\si dichos\son los dichos\y dicha sea

—footsteps—
they appear
like the fatherland appears.
Blessed the eyes
leaves
lasses
goddesses: that see it.

de pasos\se parecen\se aparece la patria.\ Dichosos los ojos\hojas\hijas\diosas: que la ven.

"Ifuelofnoforceps" 1

by Jorge Lépore

tr. Molly Weigel

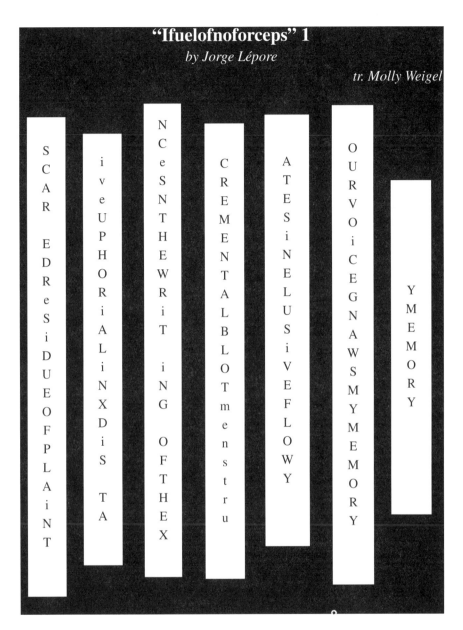

"Siamasnoforceps" by Jorge Lepore (XUL #7 p.30)
A\S\U\S\T\A\D\O\R\e\S\i\D\U\O\D\e\U\F\O\R\i\
A\L\A\M\E\N\t\o\s\a\C\O\N\E\C\T\A\L\E\\J\A\\N\
i\a\S\i\L\E\S\C\R\i\T\\U\R\A\\d\e\L\B\O\R\R\O\
N\S\E\C\E\S\i\V\O\m\e\n\s\t\r\u\a\F\L\U\J\O\
S\N\O\E\L\U\S\i\V\O\T\U\V\O\Z\M\U\E\R\D\E\L\
A\M\E\M\O\R\I\A\

"Ifuelofnoforceps" 2

```
explodedstimulinthisn
ecrophilicemergencyva
lorizingarmedisarmoni
zesvisitationsimplyin
gunioedipical)nlaconi
cal?!)visionscongesti
onofhumor'sdomitablec
aramelizedretrosucces
sivenesstrimsdifficul
tbirtharchfantasistco
ndensation)iwaited/to
dayshedidn'tcome)regu
latorylilalfalfafatte
nsaffectionatealienis
```

```
tswhispersreducinglev
itationominousfetusre
executedsenterectedpe
ripheralobsessionpush
itpullfornicatingidio
lects!)ifuckedufrombe
hindnnotbysurprise)sh
einfernsherselfpassio
natedisposablesurreal
ismkittykittykittyhab
ituationhotncoldincap
acitatedisorientedeca
pitatooyoohoocutiemix
ableballbreakingverba
lovernoverheatingcoll
```

explosionadosestímulo\snestaemergencianeco\fílicavalorizantearma\dodesarmonizavis-
itaci\onesoponiendovisiones\uniedípicas)ilacónica\?!)fluxióndumoresretr\osucesivi-
dadomitiblec\aramelizadarepodamalp\artocondensaciónarchi\fantasista)esperé/oin\ovino)a
lfalfitaprecep\tivaengordalienistasm\\imososusuralevitación\reductorafetosagorero\sre-
fusiloenvióobsesió\nalzadaperiféricaempu\jepeguetireidiolects\fornicantes)tetrascoj\oino
porsorpresa)infié\resesurrealidadpasion\aleliminablemizmizmiz\abituaciónmitimitidis\cap
acitadosdesorienta\dosdecapitantoschichí\mixtureradespijamient\orecalenturaverbalmar

ectivemarkedje   rkoffdo
seofunxpectedm   ensesma
chinationinunr   egulate
dareas)gestist   ordinal
ism)phenomenal   blockag
eflammablepani   cofmess
agesparapathyp   ossessi
vesfrombeforea   ntipsyc
hoticansiolyti   cantide
lusionalstimul   ants)lo
botomyelectroc   rashclo
rpromazinelite   rarysup
plements)patie   ntpassi
onatedeliriumc   lownica
lanxietyfetish   ism)fas
hionscreamspar   thenoge
nesis)collapsi   bleorna
mentslaxativef   ormfitt
easesbedlamjel   lyarchi
veboxestreasur   eportab
lecellsoftheli   bidonig
htmaregivespro   phylact
icmargins)shed   rawsmus
icfromhisflute   anditra
ins)toddlerize   dhabitc
onfirmingtende   ntialbo
nesthewordscon   cretiz
efictivereaderi   nahoriz
onofabricatedx   pectati
onspedestrians   orgasme

cadopajeodosis\colecti/vadinusualesme/nstruos/maqinaciónpor/áreasli/bres)ordinalis/moges
ti/sta)empachofen/oménico/pánicoquemader/odmensa/jesparapatîapo/sesivas/endantesan-
tisic/óticosa/nsiolíticosant/imaníac/os)lobotomíael/ectrocr/acclorpromanzin/asuplem/entosli
terario/s)delir/iospasionalesp/aciente/sangustiaclóni/cafetic/hismo)lamodagr/itapart/enogé-
nesis)ado/rnoscol/apsantescontor/nolaxan/tejaleamanicom/ialarch/ivocajastesorc/jaulasm/ó
vilesdlalíbid/opesadi/lladamárgenesp/reserva/tivos)ellasaca/músicad/suflautailluev/e)ábito/
sparvificadosc/onstati/votendencialue/soslasp/alabrasconcret/izanfic/tivolectornuno/rizonte/
dexpectativasa/rtefact/izadaspeatones/orgasme

ORGiNGWiTHNOJECTWHATMONKEYBiZADLEiBNiZ

NiSGASTRiCBRANCONEWiTHBATHOFLUXONANNYGO

ATGETiTKiTTYBEFOREMAKiNGTRACKSMUTiLATiNGBiL

ARGUABLECOLLOQUiALiZESiDiOCiESOFitty

OLOGEEWiZTAKiTOFFORMALiZiNG

A\M\P\A\N\S\i\N\Y\E\C\T\O\Q\U\E\M\O\N\A\D\A\D\c\h\i\c\o\S\L\E\i\B\N\i\Z\i\S\G\A\S\T\R\i\C\A\C\U\C\U\R\U\C\H\O\D\A\F\R\E\C\H\O\C\O\N\B\A\N\O\D\F\L\U\J\O\C\H\O\T\O\M\i\Z\A\N\T\E\S\M\A\R\C\A\N\D\O\V\i\A\S\M\U\T\i\L\A\N\T\E\S\B\i\L\L\C\O\N\T\E\S\T\A\B\L\E\C\O\L\O\Q\U\i\A\L\i\Z\A\i\D\i\O\T\i\S\M\O\S\D\i\C\O\i\Z\A\D\A\S\A\C\A\D\E\N\C\i\A\F\O\R\M\A\L\i\Z\A\N\T\E

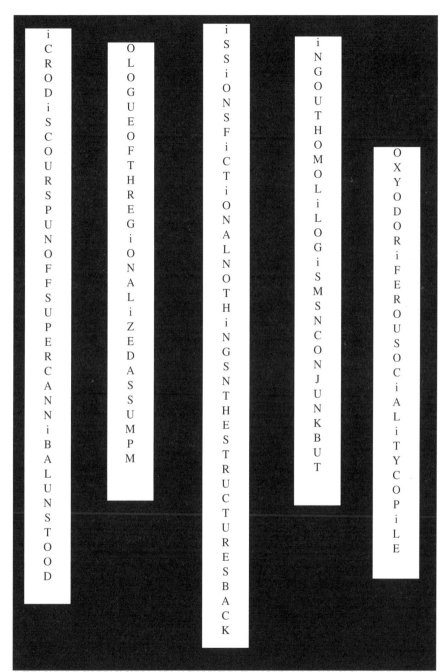

i\C\R\O\D\i\S\C\U\R\S\O\i\L\A\D\A\S\U\P\E\R\C\A\N\i\B\A\L\\O\L\O\G\A\S\U\B\T\E\N\
D\I\D\A\S\D\E\S\R\E\G\i\O\N\A\L\i\Z\A\D\A\S\U\N\M\\i\S\i\O\N\E\S\N\A\D\A\D\A\F\i\
C\C\i\O\N\A\L\E\S\i\L\A\S\E\S\T\R\U\C\T\U\R\A\S\O\M\\O\L\i\L\O\G\i\S\M\O\S\R\E\C\
U\L\A\N\T\E\S\i\A\R\T\i\C\U\L\O\P\O\S\\S\A\O\D\O\R\i\F\E\R\A\S\O\C\i\A\L\i\D\A\D\R
\E\C\O\I\o\\C\O\P

Dis
coveries
by Susana Poujol

tr. Molly Weigel

he bites the apple red watery
with those little square child's fingernails
failed pianist
unexpected ruled leaves fall from him
              he leans far back
              more and more lost
              in his long dark hair
          farther
            the voice
                        what a whorehouse
            it says
          and the voice   slips
                          between the pubic hairs
                      with my gentle persistent tongue
          what licking and licking
        at emptiness

Des / Cubrimientos by Susana Poujol (XUL #7 p.44)
muerde la manzana roja acuosa\con esas uñas cuadraditas de niño\pianista desmayado\se le
caen las hojas pautadas e improvisa\reclínase lejos\cada vez más perdido\entre sus oscuros
largos cabellos\muy lejos\la voz\qué puterío\dice\y la voz se le desliza\entre los pelos del
sexo\con mi lengua suavecita y tenaz\qué relame\el vacío

"A mate, Pacheco..."

by Susana Pujol

tr. Molly Weigel

—A *mate*, Pacheco.
Yes, my Brigadier.

—Ah...the country of apple trees...
The water flows sweetly here...all so green...

—Ne u quén...cou nt ry of ap ple trees...

Huidobro spoke of the country of the Ranqueles, Brigadier...

—Aha...but here the sun slips down through the hollows, they say... and
the apples poison themselves...
I don't know...it must be...the mountain gets angry with the intrusions...
  said the old man...
—Some little apples...from the heart of the mountain...these Indian
women with firm skin...no, Pacheco?
Do you think the mountain will get angry, Brigadier?

THE COLORADO ENCAMPMENT
Campaign to the Desert/September 1838/1983

***

Mate is a South American green tea with twice the caffeine of coffee. Neuquén is a
province to the southwest of Buenos Aires that comprises the high mountains of the
Andes and the northwest limit of the pampa. The Ranqueles were an Araucani tribe that
formerly inhabited the area of the present-day province of Neuquén.

"—un mate, Pacheco..." by Susana Pujol
—Un mate, Pacheco.\Sí, mi Brigadier.\\—Ah... el país de los manzanos...\Corre el agua
lindo aquí... todo tan verde...\\—Ne u quén... pa ís de los man za nos...\Huidobro hablaba
del país de los ranqueles, Brigadier...\\—Aha... Pero aquí el sol se descuelga por las
cañadas, dicen... y las manzanas se envenenan...\\\No sé... ha de ser... la montaña se enoja
con los intrusos... dijo el viejo...\\—Unas manzanitas... del corazón de la montaña... estas
indias de piel dura... ¿no, Pacheco?\Usté cree que la montaña se ha de enojar, Brigadier?\\
CAMPAMENTO DEL COLORADO\Campaña al Desierto /setiembre de 1838/1983

Reunion

by Hugo Savino

tr. G. J. Racz

I evoke them in the eye of night,
somewhat embarrassed,
—mine is a classifiable and somewhat sentimental shyness—
and then I beg their pardon
    (besides, I can't remember when I picked up this poem again
    and of course my melancholy is a slave to the hullabaloo of fashion
the ping! of their verses invades a number of us,
all avowedly indomitable,
    we few, we few who aspire
    to weave intrahistory!
    vacuous or grandiose
in the triangle of the folk club
                back around 1980
Anita was the mason's fairy-girl on loan.
    A motherless poppy is inconceivable,
So yellow and sweet. The countryside
            par excellence.
An allusion to drugs. Or to painting. Or
a festive epiphany. (That's more like it. Yes.) Blah. Blah.
        Blah. No, I say.
An epiphor, then.
Now the triangle regards one another amazed. Its capacity for
                [association declines.

Reunión by Hugo Savino (XUL #7 p.61)

Los evoco en el ojo de la noche,\algo avergonzado,\es un timidez clasificable y algo senti-mental\y entonces pido disculpas\(además ya no sé cuando retomé este poema\y la melan-colía está caída en el tran-tran de la moda, por supuesto)\los plin de sus versos nos invaden a unos cuantos\todos confesos, indomeñables,\unos pocos, unos pocos que aspiramos\a tejer la intrahistoria!\que vacuos o que grandiosos,\en el triángulo de la peña\allá por 1980\Anita era la fihada del albañil.\Una amapola guacha es impensable.\Es tan amarilla y dulce. El paisaje\por excelencia.\Alusión a la droga. O a la pintura. O\una epifanía festiva. (Es más posible. Es). Bla. Bla.\Bla. Digo no.\Entonces una epífora.\El triángulo ya se mira asombrado. Declina su capacidad asociativa.

One more time. Same thing. Two whiskeys and one Coca-Cola.

We speak of an absent one frightened

by these words:

"the moral and political backdrop of an era will never emerge from this."

A coward. A chicken. Another egg.

My Greek profile is sublime. But it has brought me trouble.

Something is missing between this and that. A couple of hinges, perhaps

Time passed. I delighted in my fine chançons,

and once I became aware of it they turned

from my side.

I don't know. Our women mingled and mixed.

Some tight, torn asshole over there, mild irritations.

God!

Politics again. Inflated. Inflated,

I say. I can scarcely say.

"Who knows what destiny has

in store for us?"

Let's look at some hard facts:

The pampas only shelter Studebakers,

beautiful Deckers.

Small forests are felled, the "anxiety of song" grows.

Nipponese flames. Nimbus lights. A few jazzy,

jazzy phrases. Others, others still. That

crush the bastard in that Gang.

Furtive extremes a tiny golden hand wants to unite.

There's more: Disdainful souls increase and pile up.

Otra vuelta. Lo mismo. Dos criadores y una Coca-Cola.\Hablamos de un ausente que se asusta\con estas palabras,\"de ahí nunca sale el trasfondo moral y político de una época".\Un gallina. Una gallina. Otro huevo.\Mi perfil griego es sublime. Pero me trajo algunos problemas.\Algo falta entre esto y aquello. Unas bisagritas, quizás.\Pasó el tiempo. Yo me deleitaba con mis buenas chançons,\y cuando me di cuenta se apartaron\de junto a mí.\No sé. Se mezclaron nuestras mujeres.\Algún culito roto, por ahí, suaves vejámenes.\¡Dios!\Otra vez la política. Inflada, inflada.\Digo. Apenas digo.\"Quien sabe lo que nos reserva el\ destino".\Acumulemos algunos datos:\La pampa sólo alberga algunos Studebakers,\bellos Deckers.\Se talan los bosquecitos, crece la "ansiedad de canto".\Llamas niponas. Luces nímbeas. Unas frases,\ una frases, jazzísticas. Otras, otras. Que\aplastan al bastardo de la Barra.\Extremos furtivos que una manito de oro quiere unir.\Hay más. Crecen y se amontonan las almas desdeñosas.

And soon Filippo Argenti—the supreme incarnation of evil—will be a turkey: cocky.

It's true! (To close now). I understand that he has fallen!

Off a lousy perch. But we'll get back to these ghosts.

Those in attendance on the sparse pampas are a very select class of people

who walk or show off around the neighborhoods,

wanting to know things with thin books tucked under their arms.

No one knows where he was born or the extent of his emphasis.

But one thing is certain: Radek would not look kindly on them.

"The matter of homages" unfurls

its merry-widow charms, from home

outward, sweats and earns a living.

Everyone earns a living!

Tulio Sabana

Angelus Galicoide

Don Chito Ingravallo earned one, too.

What does all this remind you of? We all know.

We all do.

Well, those of us in the métier.

We know those things, we know.

But, voilà!—on fortune's tray

lie new lies wanting to gulp down

their inventors, and then,

"those wrinkles, those stains of sin"

will be our small treasure again.

And without much courtesy we may continue

telling them:

Go to hell!

Y pronto Filippo Argenti -la suprema encarnación del mal- será un pavo:\empevesado.\Es cierto! (Y para terminar). Entiendo que se ha caído!\Desde un mísero tablón. Pero volveremos sobre estas sombras.\Los presentes de la pampa rala es una clase muy pequeña\ que camina o se muestra, queriendo saber, con un\libro delgado bajo el brazo, por algún vecindario.\Nadie sabe cuándo nació ni cual es el grado de su énfasis.\Pero algo es cierto Radek no los veía con buenos ojos.\"La tópica de los homenajes" despliega\sus encantos de viuda alegre, desde su casa,\hacia afuera, suda y se gana la vida.\Todos se ganan la vida!\Tulio Sabana\Angelus Galicoide\Se la ganaba Don Chito Ingravallo.\¿A qué suena todo esto? Todos sabemos.\Todos.\En fin, los que estamos en el métier.\ Esos, esos sabemos.\Pero-voilà!—en la bandeja de la suerte\las nuevas trolas que quieren comerse\a los inventores, y entonces,\"esas arrugas, esas manchas del pecado"\vuelven a ser nuestro tesorito.\Y sin mucha cortesía podemos seguir\diciéndoles.\¡Idos al carajo!

De Usura

(fragments)

by Reinaldo Laddaga

tr. G. J. Racz

> The most hated sort [of money-making], and with the
> greatest reason, is usury, which makes a gain out of
> money itself, and not from the natural use of it. For
> money was intended to be used in exchange, but not to
> increase at interest. And this term usury [tókos], which
> means the birth of money from money, is applied to the
> breeding of money because the offspring resembles the
> parent. Wherefore of all modes of making money this is
> the most unnatural.
>
> Aristotle, *Politics*, I, 10   *tr. B. Jowett*

ichnography:

/the setting   in between;
"on the porch"   one who says: draft, that
                          which is drafted, "slashes the
                          face," what's cut: ex-poses,
                          what hides or drafts
                          the cut, like "ichnography" or
                          passion or

                          what is crossed out, is stitched up;
                          the grimace, the moue; draft
                          or cut; intrados,
                          like "prattle,"
                          like not cut, but

De Usura by Reinaldo Laddaga (XUL #7 p.28)
ichnografía:\/puesta en cuadro\"en el pórtico"\entre;\quien dice: traza, lo\que se traza, "pinta
el\jabeque", lo cortado: ex-pone,\lo que oculta o traza\el corte, como "ichnographía"
o\pasión o\\lo que se tacha, se sutura;\la mueca, el rictus, traza\o cortado: intradós,\como
"parloteo",\como no cortado, sino

orthography:

/the setting   painted cut,
...   transposed clef,
                          cut foot:
                          what is drafted, traverses

                          or in between;

                          upright clef,
                          the intrados drafted,
                          not the floor plan, the
                          "orthographic" cut, in what's
                          painted, im-plan-ts
                          the

scenography:

/the setting   "what treads, hides track;
erasure; (curtain)   what folds, bends: unfolds,
ex-position of   unbends, hides itself;"
(the characters)   the aforesaid, (already):
                          the example: said (already)
                          "prattle," "ichnography"
                          or uproot: in what's crossed out, that
                          which stitch-like

\orthographía/puesta en cuadro\...\\pintado corte,\traspuesta clave,\cortado pie:\lo que se traza, recorre\\ o entre; armada clave\trazado el intradós,\no la planta, el corte\"orthográphico", en lo\pintado, im-planta\el\\scenographía:/puesta en cuadro\borradura; (telón)\ex-·posición de\(los personjes)\"lo que pisa, calca oculta;\lo que pliega dobla: despliega,\desdobla, ocúltase";\lo antes dicho, ya:\el ejemplo: dicho (ya)\"parloteo", "ichnographía"\o desplanta: en lo tachado, lo\que sutural

"someone ascending a staircase
is an example of a staircase;
any cut is
an example of someone
making a cut,
being cut;"

...   beneath, behind;
/the setting   beneath the (arch), behind the (arch)
"on the porch"   painted cut:
                           the intrados transposed, what's
                           painted ex-posed, im-plan-ted
                           passion ("like cut")

                           in between;

                           —at the fold, all at once:
                           of the cut (and what's) painted:
                           "prattle," "ichnography?"
                           im-plan-ted (or tracing) passion?—

"alguien subiendo una escalera\es un ejemplo de escalera;\algún corte es\un ejemplo de
alguien\haciendo un corte,\siendo cortado";/puesta en cuadro\"en el pórtico"\debajo,
detrás;\bajo el (arco), detrás del (arco)\pintado corte:\ traspuesto el intradós, lo\pintado ex-
puesto, im-plantada\pasión ("como cortado")\\entre;\\-donde el pliegue, a la vez:\del corte
(y lo) pintado:\\"parloteo", "ichnographía"?\im-plantada (o calco) pasión?

Poem

by Fabio Doctorovich

(XUL #10 p.12-13)

tr. by the author

the hellish hordes of colostrumshit at last pustulate the bribe

copulate the endorsements the marismas the gigs:

rennet spasms: condemned flies:

fucked-over flatbrains

banana power in insuflated guts

and joy

a severe dead orgasm at noon in the market's feast, the marimba players furnish buttcheeks plots embargo: [...]
cast masochist servers manifester. In Palermo: dimwitted didas dances sausage sandwiches in the square [...]
The dance is all over once the swan is dead

and bileu-green pensacola semanticizes a prosthesis

when fluffjocks chuck molasses flock-houses: a kinda bileu-blonde or piss-extract

lousy bile of those Pernambuco Rangers tentades of sargasso

filthy oracles drunk in cheap socks

punctured corks (stale wines) precede the placards the mice the bellies

superficial interventionisms. public vices obeyed by shit-for-brains

awaken and whack attack the wicked witch

a libertine's ass sucked through a tiny buried dick

August, '92, Buenos Aires
Land of Scoundrels

Dialogue Between Two Society Women

by Roberto Cignoni

tr. K. A. Kopple

—   !

—   :?

— (   ).

—   ...

— "   ."

DIALOGO ENTRE DOS SEÑORITAS DE SOCIEDAD by Roberto Cignoni
(XUL #10 p.19)

Dawnin'

by Carlos Estévez

tr. Graciela Sidoli

Th' orb
icular is 'n m'eyes 'n 'xtreme 'xpansion;
th' orb
icular is 'n m'outh 's yours;
both cartil ages 'ncreasing nasal ori fices,
and th' fingers 'n my hands: radials
an' m'ears feedin' hungry seashells,
and th' fingers n' my feet: radials,
and my body 's 'nly gram mar.

Y'r face finds astonishment 'n m' hu man'ey's.

Pop
pies, pol-
len for m'honey
(this poe-
m): retin-
al be-e
I am
in the
sun!

"AM'N'CER" by Carlos Estévez (XUL #10 p.20)
L'orbicular de 'os mios o'os 'n 'u 'xtrema 'xpansión;\l'orbicular de 'a mia boc' 'n 'u
mism' actitud;\ambos cartílagos sendos 'rificios nasales aum'ntando,\y 'os dedos 'n mis
manos: radiales,\e oreis, 'lim'ntando c'racoles h'mbrientos,\y 'os dedos 'n mis pies: radi-
ales,\y sólo gramos mi cuer'o.\\L'asombro hall a'u rostro n' mis oes humanos.\\'As
'mapol-\as, pol-\cn par' mi miel\este poe-\ma): Λbe.e-\ja retinia-\na soy\al\sol!

to wards th'blu'air climbin'
lone sun.

a cloud, a lark, climbin'
branch's laden with
in-
fin'te
ra
in.

To see,
to see soar
    a
      gain:

po,
poe,
poet
     ry.

'cia l'ait' 'zul sub!\So 'i sol.\\'na nub', av', sub' a los\ram-\ajes 'nfin'tos d' l' lluv-\ i\a.\\
Ver,\ver\rem\on\tar:\\po,\po̱e,\poes\sí\a.

Eve and the Ministers

by Andrea Gagliardi

translated by K.A. Kopple

categorical categorical categorical?

the limousine, the chauffer, the black husband
loaded up with buttons

and the Beauty
the intrepid Young girl
resting on the balcony wrinkled with seams

surrounded by enemies, by the ministers of god
she laughs, doesn't ask
doesn't hand over same coin for the useless circumstance
of loving or not

and these million people are my unfortunates
I say into his ear
as I caress him and take off his uniform

and I am yours my General

You shan't keep me from walking across the waters
from conferring authority
the names of the round earth

Eva y los ministros by Andrea Gagliardi (XUL #11 p.32)
¿categórico categórico categórico?\\la limusina, el chofer negro, el esposo negro\cargado
de botones\\ la Bella\la Joven muchacha intrépida\acodada en el balcón ajada de cos-
turas\\rodeada de enemigos, de ministros de dios\ríe, no pregunta\no da la misma moneda
por la inútil circunstancia\de amar o no\\y esos millones de gentes son mis pobres\le digo al
oído\mientras lo acaricio y le saco el uniforme\ y yo soy tuya mi General\\No querrás
impedirme que cruce las aguas caminando\que invista el mando\los nombres de la tierra
redonda

And when you choose my dirty servant's foot
to wear your shoe
I will try it on before the ladies
so that seeing me they see
the perfect fit of the queen's dreams
and all that a woman is capable of desiring

with the gold telephone you will buy me
I will speak to god
I will ask him in our need
to let us remain together in a paradise
and forgive us if we were once innocent

and to also take care of my twin sister
and the savory fruit that by his mediation I tasted

He won't punish me for that
he knows about women
how to buy the affection of a woman

I rest my lips against his tired forehead
and it is he who intercedes for me
the procession bellows at him to intercede
that I am a saint that I am She
his little virgin
with candles of the plaza and torches
in the bedrooms I will surround her

Y cuando elijas mi sucio pie de sirvienta\para colocar tu zapato\ me lo probaré delante de
las señoras\para que viéndome se vean\la medida exacta de los sueños de una reina\y todo
lo que una mujer es capaz de desear\\con el teléfono de oro que me comprarás\hablaré con
dios\le pediré por nuestra falta\que nos deje permanecer juntos en un paraíso\y nos perdone
si fuimos una vez inocentes\\y a mi hermana gemela también que la cuide\y a la fruta
sabrosa que por su intermedio probé\\No va a castigarme por eso\él sabe de mujeres\de
cómo comprar la ternura de una mujer\\Apoyo mis labios sobre su frente cansada\y es él
que intercede por mí\la procesión le grita que interceda\que yo soy santa que yo soy Ella\su
virgencita\con velas de la plaza y antorchas\en el dormitorio se la rodearé

so she protects us
and in our embrace
can do the same for all of my children

Ever since I had nothing I have been conceiving this plan
the Devil will not install himself in my body
the tumor tells me that envy exists
and Wickedness penetrates me with its horn

So that the world shall speak
the bullfighter finds pleasure and suffers
in the ring of blood

Not being buried is all that a woman desires for herself

I have nothing left
I say to the General while I transmigrate
No interest of whatever nature in anything
because now I am an Angel
— fallen — the Devil tells me

and yes

I confirm that I conserve
a sad memory
a human recollection
some form of unnecessary consideration
for others in the world

para que nos proteja\y en nuestro abrazo\poder hacerlos a todos mis hijos\\Desde que no tuve nada estoy concibiendo este plan\no vendrá el Diablo a clavárseme en el cuerpo\el tumor me dice que la envidia existe\y la Maldad me penetra con su cuerno\\Para que el mundo hable\la torera todavía goza y sufre\en la plaza de sangre\ \No ser enterrada es todo lo que una mujer desea para sí\\No me queda nada\le digo al General mientras transmigro\Ningún interés de ninguna naturaleza por nada\porque ahora soy un Angel\—caído— me dice el Diablo\\y sí\\compruebo que conservo\una triste memoria\un humano recuerdo\alguna forma de consideración innecesaria\por los otros del mundo

While I soar above the city swastika I feel
that something interests me

We pass by those neighborhoods of embraces
the little humid houses

and I love

I don't know why nor for whom the Angel tells me
Only in the negation of all action will Eve be an Angel

but I don't care for her I tell the Devil

I feel the calls of my former life
It's the General who yells at me from below
asks me to return
to rob them
to save them

And I
from this cosmic meander
above the plaza I see
the foul water fountain
the fallen birds
the broken flags
the disabled people running

the fire engines sounding off when it isn't a holiday

Mientras sobrevuelo la ciudad svástica siento\que me intereso por algo\Pasamos por aque-
llos barrios de abrazos\las casillas húmedas\\y amo\\No sé para qué ni para quién me dice
el Angel\Sólo en la negación de toda acción será la Eva un Angel\\pero no lo quiero le digo
al Diablo\\Siento los llamados de mi vida anterior\Es el General que me grita desde
abajo\me pide que vuelva\que se las roban\que se las salve\\Y yo\desde este cósmico
deambular\sobre la plaza veo\la fuente de agua maloliente\los pájaros caídos\las banderas
rotas\las gentes que corren impedidas\\a los carros de fuego sonando cuando no es fiesta

and the Devil
with his fins
drawing in the sky like an airplane

categorical categorical categorical?

y al Diablo\con sus aletas\dibujando en el cielo como un avión\ \¿categórico categórico
categórico?

Psyche

by Andrea Gagliardi

tr K.A. Kopple

unravelling the mystery with his instrument
with the first half, I'm going to assist him
by a crack of skylight pull out
the grass that confers death
I'm going to part you and you part
the woman in labor plasters the vestibule which you let me see
with the misery of cadavers
dividing up the cure
in my scab of love they see the wound
I have
great fulminating powerful
with his lance I write the poem
close it for me he said I don't want to be left alone to write
I will write on your body with my silver bone

now I search but he has gone
dressed in yellow for his destroyed soul
in the shade of the tiger I move
with infinite lines calling out to you
from the cage and the circle

Poema de Psiqué by Andrea Gagliardi
\destraba el misterio con su instrumento\en la primera mitad voy a ayudarlo\ por la hendidura del tragaluz a arrancar\la yerba que nos invista de muerte\voy a partirte y partes\la parturienta empasta los vestíbulos que me dejas ver\con la miseria de los cadáveres\\reparte la curación\ en mi costra de amor ven llaga\tengo una\ gran poderosa fulminante\con su lanza inscribo el poema\dijo ciérramela no quiero quedarme solo a escribir\voy a escribir sobre tu cuerpo con mi hueso de plata\\ahora lo busco pero se fue vestido\de amarillo para su alma destrozada\en la sombra del tigre me muevo\con trazo infinito llamándote\dentro de la jaula y del círculo

Poem to Eros

by Andrea Gagliardi

tr K.A. Kopple

because of god's having done me evil in uneven parts
because of the devil's order that governs me
I lay down on the sand to wait for him and said to him
that in order to return he had to change
in his idiotizing meanings I found the solution
and in his crippled rib the envy that drives the world crazy

because I had cruelty in my bones
I treated him like a dog and he with my beauty looked at me
I would not give it to you were it not
that it overflows my recipient and you take it from me

he came to the seventh to speak to me about everything he had done
with his destiny and obligation to fulfill
I didn't draw the veil and wrapped his flesh
with the shroud that holds the cranium
I endured the cry of his tentacle for my conduct

Poema a Eros by Andrea Gagliardi
\por haberme hecho dios el mal en partes desiguales\por mandato del diablo que me gobierna\me acosté en la arena a esperarlo y le dije\que para volver tenía que cambiar\en sus idiotizados sentidos encontré el remedio\y en su costilla lisiada los celos que enloquecieron al mundo\\porque tenía ensañamiento con mis órganos\lo traté así como un perro y él con mi belleza me miró\no te la daría si no fuera\que excede mi recipiente y me la quitas\\vino al séptimo a hablarme de todo lo que había hecho\con su destino y su condena a hacer\no corrí el velo y contuve su carne\ con la mortaja que atrapa el cerebro\soporté el grito de su tentáculo por mi conducto

because of the decision of Fury I wanted to see
with lamp and with lanze the covering of his brain
his worm managed to introduce itself
into the enigma with the question
and upon leaving had already punctured me

I ceased hearing the burnt voice before escaping together with his mother

por decisión de Furia quise ver\con lámpara y con lanza el revestimiento de su cráneo\su gusano consiguió metérseme\en el enigma con la pregunta\y al salir ya me había agujerea-do\\dejé de oír la voz quemada antes de escapar junto a su madre

Optical Ashes (fragments)

by Raúl García

tr by K.A. Kopple

Arms agitate unmasking
(try it) a beating of wings
flaying. Great wings
purple splinters of bats
rub like heavy pendulums
rags becoming light and shadows
rubbing

Air that floats
the simulacrum
the body image of Lucretius
push air to force the pupil
(emit the eye making it explode warping
the mirror's silvery surface
send our eye on the rebound:
inverse image

Crystaline air
Transparencies,
beauty
of vitriol
She splits,
contracting.
Splits

Cenizas Opticas (fragmentos) by Raúl García (XUL #11 p.31)
Brazos agitar desembrozando\(inténtanlo) un batir de alas\despelleja. Aletones\morados astillas de murciélagos\frotan como péndulos pesados\Trapos a ser luz y sombras.\Estregadura.\\Aire que flota\el simulacro…\cuerpo de la imagen de Lucrecio\ empuja aire para chocar la pupila\(emite el ojo haciéndola estallar chapuceando\la superficie plateada el espejo\envía en rebote nuestro ojo:\inversa imagen.\\Aire cristalino.\Transparencias,\belleza\de vitriolo.\Ella raya,\ crispando.\Raya.

Eden,
        interlaces the voices
        screwed into the copper
        crystal; how much the "ideas"
of the Bishop Berkeley, vociferate
the naming (word) point of composing
flesh out of things
which substance is it that links
in the puddle of ashes
or auric shavings the bodies?
the action? the axiomatic:
apogee of the vision fading away
the eye
      the apex.

Prism, specterscope
open fan of colors
this explosion!
injures the gasping iris
reverse sides, cage
of the beaten gaze
Curves changing upon
swelling

How many?

    (...)

Edén,\entrelaza las voces\atornilladas al cristal\cobrizo; cuanto las "ideas"\del obispo Berkeley, vocifera\la nominación (palabra) punto a componer\pellejo de las cosas\¿cuál la sustancia que engarza\en charco de cenizas\o virutas áuricas los cuerpos?\¿la acción? La axiomática:\auge de la visión desvaneciéndose\el ojo\ el vértice.\\Prisma, espectroscopio\ abanico abierto de colores\¡ese estallido!\lástima el iris reboqueado\enveses, jaula\de mirada curtida\Ajustando curvas al\envararse\cuántos?\(...)

As if on the run
the sperm wiggles.

Crippled puppets, accordion the
swollen satres at
the eyelid's inner wall
project; little filiform shadows
spheres
the little trembling twigs and
frolicking sweat speckled from the
vitreous humor: *muscae volitants*
flecks. (they fall
Gestures, theatre (glassy)
private gaze
Miles of tiny mouths
mouthing without words,
without crepe tongues
intestines to lick
loose and curvy.

Theatreye. (*Palpebrals*).

On the run the semen
wiggle.
Snake.
Split.

Como a la carrera el esperma\se menean.\\Títeres tullidos, acordeón los\sátiros envarados a\la pared interna del párpado\proyecta; sombritas filiformes\esferas\los bastoncillos temblequeando y\brincan sudores moteados del\humor vítreo: muscae volitantes\flecos. (caen\Gestos, teatro (vidrioso)\ privado la mirada.\Millares de boquitas\boquean sin palabras,\sin lenguas crepés\tripas a lamer\sueltas y encorvadas.\\Teatrojo. (Palpebrales).En carrera el semen\se menea.\Serpentea.\Rayan.

The protuberance in brown smoke.
Agglomeration of cloth
moist globe organizes the
luminicous chaos, this crude circulation
of rays in floods
snow and night
open the *crenha hymenea*
the naked things.

From there spirals leave and
there was eye.

La protuberancia en humos pardos.\Aglomeración de tejido\globo mohoso organiza el\caos lumínico, esa circulación\cruda de rayos en aluviones\nieve y noche\abrir las crencha himenea\las cosas desnudas.\\De allí espiras parten y\hubo ojo.

The Golfer's Discourse

by Ernesto Livon Grosman

tr. K. A. Kopple

Of the origin in question
they say to her they say
are they - now are they - were they?
from another voice surfaces this time
goes forward and other
times makes the question
inquire as to an answer
approaching to surprise
     the neighbors sees them coming
the neighbors feel alarmed and form doubts
the debts exhaust themselves and form inquisitors
once upon a time we were Ukranians, Romanians, Germans, dwarves
with time we became
nevertheless you don't or it or understand
the Charruas to the distant eye
the inquisitor at the raised hand's perspective
looking for the ginkos your merciful ones lost against the sound of
                              the water
an extinction, the ginko's, that foretells others, the ego's?
and the only member of an entire half a family
of whom but only one best sees the relation,

El Discurso Del Golfista by Ernesto Livon Grosman (XUL #11 p.34)
La pregunta es por el origen\le dicen ella le dicen \¿son — están — fueron?\de otra voz
surge esta vez\se adelanta y otras\veces hacen a la pregunta\inquirir para una respuesta\se
acercan por sorpresa\se los veía venir\los vecinos\los vecinos se alarman y formulan
dudas\los deudos se agotan y formulan inquisidores\en un principio éramos ucranianos,
rumanos, germanos, enanos\con el tiempo devenimos\sin embargo usted no o lo o
entiende\los charrúas en el ojo ajeno\el inquisidor en la perspectiva a mano alzada\que bus-
car ginkos que sus mercedes perdieron contra el sonido del\agua\una extinción, la del
ginko, que presagia otras, ¿la del ego?\y es el único miembro de toda una media
familia\que mejor único que aquel que ve la red,

undistracted
the cloud on the wooden table
holes filled with monks planting
the side of a road that, who waters?
in the origin there's more than one name, two at least

Maidenhair, coriander or...
in the beginning there are names
almost superfluous to describe them
when they can be observed so easily
and their properties being as familiar as they are
nevertheless they confuse, confuse us
the fragility of our names
is the fog of our confusion?
there is an end, no names
Linus saying so long passes by
in a hurry
we haven't had time to respond

I

let him open, the space opens
pushes the walls of earth
the gaps of light don't leave
   room for the mountain

a leafy bottomless gap
   all within

que no se distrae\la nube en la mesa de madera\agujeros llenos de monjes plantadores\orilla
de un camino que ¿quién riega?\en el origen hay más de un nombre, por lo menos
dos\\Maidenhair, culantrillo o ...\en el comienzo hay nombres,\casi superfluo
describirlos\cuando se pueden observar con tanta facilidad\y sus propiedades son tan cono-
cidas como lo son\sin embargo se los confunde, se nos confunde\la fragilidad de nuestros
nombres\¿es la niebla de nuestra confusión?\hay final, no nombres\Lineo nos dice adiós al
pasar\con la velocidad\no hemos tenido la oportunidad de responder\\I\\dejar que él abra, se
abra al espacio\empujar las paredes de tierra\los agujeros de la luz que no dejan\lugar para
la montaña\un agujero frondoso sin fondo\todo adentro

without or empty
the... constructing in the plain that included
very old mountains
(not sacred, what makes a sacred mountain is on the other side
of waters that we cross but forget)
after coming out of a dream without any more they realized that what
was, that what that, moved with them
was the mountains at the side of the cloud
the deer below
the window a small smudge against the air
taking care of the great shutters in the wind
agitating the eucaliptus
stirring the chimney in the rear
there's no possible distortion that isn't work
or a task done, inadvertantly completed
without mark *or its absence*
a stream surrounding the habitat
planting what wasn't
taking more than twenty years
painting against nature
a ceaseless moment... tiring
Never entirely at ease
he said to the maid
    "I plant eucaliptus so the swimmers will have shade"

sin o vacío\la... construir en la llanura que incluía\montañas viejísimas\(no sagradas, que lo que hace una montaña sagrada está al otro\lado\de una agua, la cruzamos pero nos olvidamos)\después de salir de un sueño sin resto ni se dieron cuenta\que lo habían, que lo que, se movía con ellos\eran las montañas a lomo de nube,\los ciervos abajo\una pequeña mancha la ventana contra el aire\cuidar de los postigones en el viento\soliviantar el eucalipto\revolver la chimenea en el fondo\no hay distorsión posible que no sea trabajo\o simplemente otro trabajo\o una tarea hecha, inadvertidamente cumplida\sin marca «or its absence»\un arroyo alrededor del hábitat\plantó lo que no estaba\tomó más de veinte años\pintar contra la naturaleza\un momento que no cesa.... cansa\Nunca acostumbrado del todo\le dijo a la sirvienta:\"siembro eucaliptos para que los bañistas tengan sombra"

A gesture against the grain
   against the grass, when it's not growing well.

They came looking for him late
found him drinking coffee next to the car
smoking with a farmhand who works in the sheds

this isn't easy
no it isn't
in this and that year (...)
a type
there
on an island
there far away
created a game
they play it in a different way
the other plays it
here,
on the green
   between the benches
not between me
   between him
a destiny
the same old destiny

                               a game I believe
                               is watched
                               without chance
                               not a cause

Un gesto contra pelo\contra pasto, cuando está mal\\Lo vinieron buscando tarde\lo encontraron tomando café al lado del auto\fumando con un peón que trenza en los galpones\\esto no es fácil\no es\en tal y cual año (...)\un tipo\allá\en una isla\allá lejos\construye un juego\lo juegan de otra manera\el otro juega\aquí,\en los greens\entre bancos\no entre mí \entre él\un destino\el mesmo destino\un juego creo\que se mira\sin azar\no una causa

but an identity
another origin

in a beginning
      some are golfers
          artists
          baptists

what a descent that of the golfer's
that ascent without touching the little thing
that holds up the ball
... that discourse! that of this guy
it's not just, nor logical, nor enough
it's not a discourse but a point of view
that the house still hasn't been fixed
distractions of the origin that haven't end nor solution
since then he couldn't make it up the hill to the restaurant
and said that in this country what
is needed
      doesn't
         e
             x
                i
                    s
                        t
                  anymore
                  (it's only a point of view)

sino una identidad\otro origen\\\en un principio\algunos son golfistas\artistas\bautistas\\que descenso el del golfista\que ascenso sin tocar el cosito ese que sostiene la pelota\¡...discurso ese! el del tipo este\no es justo, ni lógico ni suficiente\no es discurso sino un punto de vista\que la casa aun no ha sido reparada\distracciones por el origen que no tienen fin ni arreglo\desde que ya no podía subir la cuesta del restaurante\y decía en este país lo que se necesita\no\e\x\i\s\t\e\ya más\(es sólo un punto de vista)

II

Don't mix things up more
or you lose
Leonidas Lamborghini

finding yourself lost
finding yourself green
outside the house
you go to the sheds
you mix more and more up
with those things
of that kind over there in the distance
here the women to the north and
to the south of the terrain a book of notes
a list against all losing oneself
beside the firewood,
       more firewood,
       a pack of cigarettes in three days
       a long discourse about the economy
       two hours
       a map of the subway systems,
       discussing the housing in Harlem
       or before Harlem
       or after the park
       stories of and by the mail

II\No mezclés más las cosas\o te perdés\Leónidas Lamborghini\te perdés\te verdés\en las afueras de la casa\te vas para los galpones\te mezclás más y más\con las cosas de este\tipo allá al fondo\acá las mujeres al norte y\al sur del terreno un libro de notas\una lista contra todo perderse,\al costado de la leña,\más leña,\una caja de cigarros en tres días\una larga perorata sobre la economía\dos horas\un mapa del sistema de subterráneos,\discutir sobre la vivienda en Harlem\o antes de Harlem\o después del parque\historias de y por correo

....

Ah! don't leave us golfer
a chorus of wives say
and not because of a little appearance
or much playing around
desperation about what hangs powerless
among the little mountains of golfers
powerless,
idiots
retards
hands full
running after a little ball they scarcely see
now that there aren't any heroes to kill,
ranchers cross the sea of cows
let's do it
let's do it for tomorrow we die
            ___ it's a lovely country
            ___ this is my country
                   my country club

....

wandering about to see him move
in and out of the light
let in by the recently opened doors
emptying one ashtray after another
10 am in the sound of a truck that passes en route when it
has

....\"Ah! no nos dejes golfista"\dice un coro de
esposas\y no por poca desaparición\ni mucha monta\desesperación del que cuelga sin
poder\entre montañitas de golfistas\sin poder,\idiotas\retardados\las manos llenas\persigu-
iendo una pelotita que casi no ven\como ya no hay héroes que matar,\alimentadores de
vacas\cruzan el mar de vacas\a coger\a coger que se chocan las europas__es un país her-
moso...__this is my country,\my country club\..\
hacer el peregrinaje para verlo moverse\dentro y fuera de la luz\que entra con la excusa
de\los postigones recién abiertos\que vacía un cenicero detrás dc otro\10 am en el sonido
de un camión que pasa en la ruta cuando se\ha

been waiting for sunrise since 6 and she says
Hi Dear! Would you like a mate?
Iforgotyoudon'ttakesugarthey'rebiscuitsonthetable
at noon he searches for his the temperature, water, tank of the
light they look for its point of overflow 2pm deliberating about where to go
3pm get wood   4pm coffee 5pm mate 6pm trip into town
to the countrystore
first warming up the trip
the conversation drinks up while
we stop at the bank
to see the creek rise
to the countrystore
we don't move
turn down the radio
look at the river
bread/wine/cigarettes/newspaper)
in the countrystore
(meat/diesel/cheese/biscuits)
....

Dear Father I tell you that
Why do you always "run" to the post-office?
I want you to know that you seem heavier
short, forgetful, right-handed, worse at making tea, better ... etc.

estado esperando el amanecer desde las 6 y ella dice\pasá querido ¿querés un mate?\meolvidabaquetomásinazucaralláenlamesatenésgalleta\el mediodía busca su la temperatura, el agua, el tanque de\la\luz buscan su punto de llenado 2pm deliberar hacia donde ir\ 3pm traer leña 4pm café 5pm mate 6pm viaje al pueblo\al estanco\precalentado el viaje\la conversación se abreva mientras\ paramos a la orilla\para ver subir el arroyo\hacia el estanco\no nos movemos\bajamos la radio\miramos el río\pan/vino/cigarrillos/diario)\en el estanco\(carne/diesel/queso/galletitas)\..
\Querido Papá te cuento que\Why do you always "run" to the post-office?\Quiero que sepas que te encontré más gordito,\petiso, olvidadizo, diestro, peor cebador, mejor...etc.

The pscyhologist discharged either me or her
Would you sell everything? And then?
It's as though you were physically close and distant
as if you were physically And spiritually
we are left more uncertainties
It is like somebody coming back from a long trip
I think that it's not a family
I think I don't have any family
These days we all sleep inside
Waiting for snapshots, of You, yours, goodbye

>with summer gone
>we all want to see them
>they never cease looking at th
>we don't know when

You forgot a card
A book behind the bed

Please send catalogue,
including listings on anthropology,
psychology,
baseball
and sports literature, aikido
t'ai chi chu'uan, holistic health and general medicine,
embryology, midwifery, karate, and alchemy. No charge
if included with order. 75C separately.

A mí o a ella la psicóloga nos dio de alta\Would you sell everything? And then?\Es como si estuvieras cerca físicamente y lejos\como si fueras físicamente Y espiritualmente\nos van quedando más incertidumbres\It is like somebody coming back from a long trip\I think that it's not my family\I think I don't have any family\En estos días todos dormimos adentro\Esperamos fotos, de Ustedes, suyos, afuera\con la ida del verano\todos queremos verlos\no dejen de mirar en l\que no sabemos cuando\ \Te olvidaste una tarjeta\Un libro detrás de la cama\Please send catalogue,\including listings on anthropology,\psychology,\ baseball\and sports literature, aikido,\t'ai chi chu'uan, holistic health and general medicine,embryology, midwifery,karate, and alchemy. No charge if included with order. 75C separately.

A force where nature
is a second intuition

the mass of property
security in one's pocket

lost
in empty constructions

in houses full

I believe that I've now given
a brief account

an idea of our life
kisses,

                          Buenos Aires isn't Europe
                          Brooklyn in a bathrobe
                   Sierra de la Ventana isn't Buenos Aires
              better yet the province with distance in between
              the sierras, there were many years in between
                 among us, elevations throughout the trip
        at the surprise of returning to see them rise up one understands
                     that absence brings the surprise back
                   I could pay my rent and once I lent him
                                            money
                        a city in the south he was taken to
                                            by car

Una fuerza donde la naturaleza\es una segunda intuición\\la unidad de la propiedad\soltura
en el bolsillo\\pérdida\en construcciones vacías\\en casas llenas\\creo que ya hice\un
pequeño raconto\\una idea de nuestra vida\besos.\\Buenos Aires no es Europa\Brooklyn en
robe de chambre\Sierra de la Ventana no es Buenos Aires\mejor la provincia con distancia
de por medio\las sierras, había muchos años de por medio\entre nosotros, elevaciones a lo
largo del viaje\la sorpresa de volver a ver-las asomar se entiende\que la ausencia nos
devuelve la sorpresa\podía pagar mi alquiler y una vez le presté\plata\una ciudad al sur de
la sierra lo llevaba en\auto

investing in the purchase wasn't a
waste
he looked at her looking at a horizon of clouds
and trucks
someone had to tend the fire and close the
windows
we waited for playtime, to play
dice

a foot sleps
without much effort
looking at reality through only one eye
and before they both shut
it's another trip
a silence
on your birthday

Movement, he who watches

The absence of snow
has taken away the ice

the pool water
is a game played by children
for other ....ed
children

fire xxxinxxx arms
a principle cause

la inversión de la compra no fue un\desperdicio\la miraba a ella que miraba un horizonte de
nubes y camiones\alguien tenía que alimentar el fuego y cerrar las ventanas\esperábamos la
hora de jugar, de los\dados\un pie se resfala\sin mucha presión\mira a la realidad de un ojo
sólo\y antes que se cierren los dos\es otro viaje\un silencio\en su cumpleaños\Movimiento,
el que mira\\La ausencia de nieve\se ha llevado el hielo\\el agua de la pileta\es un juego de
niños\\para otros niños\...............ados\\fuegos xxxenxxx brazos\un primer motivo

mechanism of something
in the terrain deserted because of winter

a regiment of trees
passes by

there is no visible story
only

on this parcel of land
where you're poorly stopped

paternity leaves
behind

ahead
"so much water"
an archiplication
         lakes

motor de algo\en el terreno desierto por el invierno\\pasa un regimiento\de árboles\\no hay
historia visible\sólo\en este pedazo de terreno\donde estás mal parado\\la paternidad
deja\por detrás\ \por delante\"tanta agua"\un archipliegue\lagos

I looked back
from my cabin door,
to where he would close the door
and I was left outside
and said,
"this is it, it's over,
there's no more now."
If I don't move in the door. . .
if the door doesn't move
but an owl appeared from among the beams
When I return home
not to this one (which I have yet to open)
nor the one in the city so far away
no, nor to the other one in which I no longer live
but the one near the river
before I moved to the one so close
that resisting is only common sense
(before I return to the country)
when I get home I am going to write
several times, one over another
over the other.
I went in, left the door open

Miré hacia atrás\desde la puerta de mi cabaña,\hacia donde él cerraba la puerta\y me quedé afuera\y dije:\"esto es todo, se acabó,\ya no más."\Si no me muevo en la puerta,\si la puerta no se mueve...\pero un búho salió de entre las vigas\Cuando vuelva a mi casa,\no a esta (que aun no abro)\ni tampoco a la de esta ciudad tan lejos\no, no tampoco a la otra en la que ya no vivo\sino a la que está cerca del río,\antes de que me mude a la que está tan cerca\que resistir es sólo sentido común\(ante de que vuelva a la frontera)\cuando vuelva a casa lo voy a escribir\varias veces, una sobre otra\sobre la otra.\Entré, dejé la puerta abierta

THE EDITORIALS

Issue #4.

> but the froward tongue shall be cut out.
>
> Proverbs 10,31

In response to the siege, XUL felt it necessary to beseige the same question from two different and corollary perspectives: translation and illegibility.

To translate is to work in one language from another. Translating is the linguistic exercise that most privileges the breach between two texts because it is actually a previous reading that produces a new text in which writing claims to make a former text legible even as it disrupts and obfuscates one text by subtracting from it a legibility that it confers on another.

A translation that in practice tries to suppress this breach between two texts by basing itself in the rigor of a system of equivalences acts as a mirage. In its wish to decant spirits, it leaves off where it began: trying to demonstrate its efficacy in mediumistic sessions, good and far removed from the texts, functioning only as a diversionary technique. Translation only acquires significance, as far as XUL is concerned, when it affirms itself as a writing process that voluntarily exhibits its relation to other texts.

Illegibility, always partial, makes it impossible for the reader to produce the meanings of a text. But absolute illegibility does not exist and, besides that, it in and of itself is not about a definite, final situation. No text is illegible forever. Decodification and analysis, concrete experience with the text, reverses the situation.

XUL's commitment to reality is actually a commitment to language: to again make legible that which has been used for coercion and deception. Language belongs to everyone. Moreover, its ever changing form is the product of the community's collective efforts. Nonetheless, the community cannot make certain uses of the product of its efforts. It has no voice with which to give meaning to the vote. The discursive practice is monopolized.

Under the state's direct or indirect dominion and perpetuating the military autocracy, the mass media (if the analogy is valid) produced its translation in order to make its reality illegible. Similarly, with the end of assuring that the mechanism of this illegibility would not be discovered, it proceeded to protect the official translation from other versions of reality. It suppressed all translations with which it was in conflict.

But the illegibility of a text, or its suppression, are not eternal. Finally, at the same time that the media's triumphant discourse came apart little by little due to the contradictions between facts and utterances, the trick of the intentional cover-up was uncovered. The great symptom of the decomposition of a discourse, as a reading of reality, is produced when its lie becomes legible.

"Who shut the gate on words?" XUL murmured, without seeing that inside was don Fierro and with him...

tr. K.A. Kopple

Issue #6
Were So Many Lobotomies Necessary In Order To Quell So Little Flabby Content?

A contemporary publication puts out an issue about Girondo just like an issue about the mechanism of ex-xul-tation, that is to say, an issue of Xul: constructions and deconstructions of some ex-xul-ted bodies, open textures. The ex-xul-ted, product of the mechanism of ex-xul-tation, reproduces itself. It spins and spins the pedal and stoics, lotus eaters, sychophants, pass through the sieve, reflecting and speculating like the law of the Literary Arcadia. Deep within our flabby selves, we're all Egyptians; therein lies Girondo, not only in the flabby content. The ex-xul-ted is a false remedy against Egyptophobia. The spynx of exile feigns an enigma but cannot feign (exist) within the apodictic mode that affirms its reason for existing in that which, although subjects can be inverted or changed, forms part of the same predicating order, the same syntax of days gone by and combative metaphors which become more and more pronounced. With a shift, the enigma vanishes; the enigma stops feigning. What the enigma obfuscates is the discursive battle for the occupation of a territory from which no one emerges from the geographic or casuistic order. It's always about despotic variants, a rapid change of investitures, the topic of the exiled to exile.

In a concentractionary context, the contemporary publication thinks that suffrage signifies the possibility of returning to a juridical civil order without abandoning criticism to the system of options imposed by a previous judgement, which includes, tautologically speaking, systematized precedents, judgements, impositions and options. A massive conversion to stoicism that palpitates in the meteorological ontology occurs prior to the germination of liquids ("bellum"). After nearly tens years of marriage, she learns that he - a Lycian soldier - had an incunabulum of Solon's. Do Lycia and Solon feel the same? The one not cheering is an Epicurean? Is it the old trick of wanting to say everything according to the hypnotic criteria used by advertising? Things forge themselves in order to be read; an espectorating vitalism all in pursuit of a massphoto.

Lobotomy and Literature (old beliefs, one will say, reappear in a contemporary publication). The proof of Girondo's existence also affirms itself in an absence: that of the levelling utterance of the mass media. "I haven't even the desire to have the statue's blood. I don't claim to suffer the humiliation of the sparrows. I don't want anyone to drool on my grave with common places, since the only really interesting thing is the mechanism of feeling and thinking. Proof of existence!" This absence finally returns certain rationalizations, some political, various aesthetic - all of them ex-xulted - to the atopic bodies that cannot be included in the lobotomized ratio whose mechanism is the only proof of its existence, the reduplication ad infinitum of the paralyzing illustrious metaidiocy on the part of subjects that feel threatened and persecuted by a lack of restraint. Was it necessary to use so many disabled commuter buses to gather together stoics, sychophants, lotus eaters, jesuits, spartans, etcetera, and Egyptians in order to take them nowhere?

tr. K.A. Kopple

Issue #7
Poetic Campaign to the Desert–Critique–of the
Disabled Commuter Buses

Enough of Conquests! We're tired of winning.

"The desert is that which is not certus." That which is uncertain is that which has no certainty. From that which is uncertain there cannot be constructed a system or norm—but what is uncertain can be excluded by the norm: the norm it names as des-certus. Namely, is a zebra a stripped horse or a horse a plain zebra? And then, why does the janitor call the zebra a stripped horse and the maid, the horse a plain zebra, if both of them ride on the same consortium? Hachoo, it's not a consortium, it's a consensus, the goat sneezed, not the zebra, and the janitor and maid replied in chorus, "The goat doesn't know anything ... It's a foppish animal."

In order to perpetuate their calvary, the janitor and the maid generate the desert that, to conceal itself, generates the Album of Argentine Culture that, to fill it, repeatedly generates the cardboard figures of the little Argentine man that, in its articulation, generates the idolatrous gesture toward the heroic names that, to sustain the order of the Album's register, generates its transformation into lifelong pseudonyms. It's shot to hell that which, in its turn, sustains the fluxuating sign of the wimpy alienist, that same old guy, down the hall and to the right of the Album. And either by lobotomy or straight jacket or a pacifier of insulin, I beg them "let me administer a little to myself please." The Album projects the standard happiness of the court, that consortium of Cinderellas that dance until midnight, eat partidges, live happily ever after.

The desert is believed to be the kingdom of mineral, of pure stillness, of luminous and empty vibrations. Wrong. There reigns an impossible and immortal life: the life of the body itself. Blasphemers or heretics, all of the objects of Justinian etymological passion—isn't that our Emperor?—for whom the right to terrorize is law. But the goat, the animal with only one hump, cannot be confused with the poor devils who scheme up clerical ideology: Veni Domini Felix. They're here! They're here! No anus to shit, no mouth to suckle. Very well, some other hole then. Either they wanted each other, don't want each other, will want each other. They'll live happily ever after.

tr. K.A. Kopple

121

Issue #9
Editorial: Letter to the President

Dear Doctor,

There is a world that has disappeared in a certain well of frozen humours: a world of country, family, science, justice and religion which establishes itself daily and whose inhabitants allow, or pretend to allow, conscience to remit them to an excentric commandment, the call or versicle of a certain notion which doesn't correspond to anything real but spares them the atrocious suffering of having to question that conscience at its very core. There is also another world, an eternally pilfered hide out that unceasingly sheds its masturabatory rages, upright in the intersection of phenomena, and which unconditionally surrenders to a certain terrifying fold that is not imprisoned by humanity through custom: the world hurdled in a sigh by a genital scream like a natural law. Between these surfaces, a spiritual spike juts out that nails us to the center of the form, trying to surrender us without piety to being torn rectally apart by both principles: evidently, by the blows of abortion and by that which the body stores up in the pain of being quartered by the insoluble traction of those centripital forces, irreducible by whatever means to an example of the stability of consciousness. Poetry is born in the vital differentiation, and for nothing scholarly, between both dominions which allows those soluble elements of natural pulsations to be reintroduced into society by an exploded and unitary language, the gesture at once topological and marked in the absurdity of a fundamental rejection, of a material at the limit of an encision. We would have preferred to live in a state of detachment, of fierce indifference with respect to determined conceptions and packages, retaining at every moment a mobile and equidistant position in an area of circumference inhibited by the appetites and earthly gods. But they gave birth to us by the womb and not the spirit in order to bring us forth by an infection of vaginal canonfires and a below where they heap together the anchors and the extra weight of a certain positive intermission charged with inciting that retarded part of our being that impelled itself to rid us of an infinite possibility. The world has not stopped getting harder, becoming more of a drag, because of its abstract opacity and the masses which conform to it. And, at any rate, some have preferred to visit a reality which does not lead to schools or temples of edible carton since, in the end, it doesn't work by sustaining the nausea of commitment but the vibratile cilium of things and the odor of the unutterable.

What speaks on the pedestal of the void, what does not want to be employed for a gravitating interpretation, what conceives its objects admist the laws of the illogical and the non-laws of Logic and, at the same time, it conceives them, loses them, what the entire craneum of bad demencia terminates by this strange intelligence is the only thing that fraternizes the world in the flightiness of its meaning that provokes a stentorian laugh to veer, a laugh of an exhaled viscera that if it transforms itself into a murderer is only because of the intervention and the plan of the parasitic agents of a Regime.

Being in this world, respected Doctor, consists of a greater acceptance than that of living in society. I refer to a certain commotion by which our actions should consecrate themselves to recreate without exception the hidden and innate being of thought.

I don't know of another monstrous creature but that which fabricates a perpetual adaptation always on its way back to itself, a language applied to the seal of representation and an ideological rhythm that prevents it from rising to a certain astronomical geography by shying away from the Idea. All of this viscous tide of beings called the people and of which contagion constitutes an inescapable boundary had not breathed any more than to kneel before life and to flee the making of a contradictory body: a body released from its fetichistic character that accepts measuring itself with the badly formulated word and with the confused word on the frontiers of a void.

Flesh from which all reality has been sucked out, affixed to the indefinite multiplication of things—thoughts that awaken in these things and throws overboard the idiotizing anguish of a subjective annihilation that decompresses as much the fixating cholera of repressions as this socio-familiar machinery destined to perpetually reproduce submissive organisms.

This moral expansion of nothingness is only achieved by some wisemen and some mentally ill while the rest constitutes itself in a troop of disguised exploiters that propose as possible to compose existence with individuality, charisma, the trajectory or the perimeter.

In the interstices of these words, respected Doctor, you no doubt wished to extract us from the marrow since what emerges implicates you without rodeos in an enervating quality: a quality which doesn't consume itself in the mafioso intrigues of an earthly cacoon but in the premeditated castration before a metaphysical dive.

If this should not happen as such, please have the goodness to teach us with but one of your words that has not been pronounced in order to avail itself, one of your gestures that has not wished to contribute to a mythology, one of your acts that did not attempt to fill a fluid territory and was not engendered for the occupation.

You are not monstrous for having corrupted the political order even more, devastating until saturation an opaque block with a puppet totem but for having risen above the distressed and uneducated masses in order to investigate life itself without having disinterred one single time the marrow of your glove, then overturning the center of not one single thing the absolute heart of copulating, kicking, urinating and tossing and turning until all of that moves with the rejected and the unrevealed exposing of yourself by a single gesture and a vast sigh.

On the other hand, you have entrusted yourself to crossing out this physiological drama that allows man to remake himself, elevating yourself by a kneaded pore and a diction spit out without contraction as if the hydrocarbons of a feeling permitted the economization of the distance, as if what is cast by a signified wind could recompose the audacious and perplexed state of mind, as if what again moved the syllables through a created interest were capable of provoking the profound sexuality or the form's incessant swell. This chain of fabricated rictus that the televised and journalistic images impose on us daily has not ceased to act like an electroshock over the spirit's revolutionary expansions and now cannot perceive society as anything but a pantagruelistic hospice over which a perfect imbecil, who has lost the key to his organic experience, has authority soon to redeem his pedestal before the formidable dais that spoils a paralyzed blood.

Doctor, you should know that we have never given you the right to freeze these spinning lands where the exalted spirit of man transforms itself ceaselessly and which you, slithering in banal syllogisms and contractions of personal defense, propose to inventory.

Now, it's no longer conceivable to acquiesce your public custom of turning your back on the drama of a shameless relief, always reinitiated in the profound fabric of being, in order to cuff, with an urgent justification, your unreconcilable social contradictions to those instinctive fits that, in the end, permit a magical identification with the collective humours of man.

It's no longer possible for our theater of exploration to tolerate your august, formal and, always, inspected mask of opportunism that has been displaced from the political instance of man's character until devouring this illuminating blossom by which we should understand that life has been offered to direct us toward the totality of founding ourselves with.

You have not wished to take upon yourself the energetic job of sounding out more than a-b-c so that all of those people, whose only language comes from the stereotypical and only allow themselves to look to a public power that shall never be born while you put into practice that which implies blocking the voltaic shifts and errant options of the spirit-word, the perception-word and the absolute free-game.

Understand us well: this is not the cry of moralists hidden under a civilian mask like the lawyers of a whiny civil society that accuses you of not keeping your promises, of yielding to demagogery, of being disposed to deny whatever to conquer and conserve your power. Such contraventions, used by the most adept in order to avoid obstacles and overcome blocks and the most cowardly to grovel with whoever to perpetuate an empire, make themselves at home in the very breast of our amiable republican mechanisms.

A fucking camouflage of antidogmatism and flexibility becomes to a magistrate what mineral is to a rock; and we commit a substantial error if we hammock before this subculture with its idealistic rag of that which is transparent or the graces of a Golden Age in which man, transformed into pure desire, takes himself in.

No burden awaits you because of the alliances and blackmail among powerful elites in the sanctuaries of the public theater, because of the crustation of, like courtly ornaments, poetry and music, because of those totalitarian enterprises that rub their means together in order to form circumstantial opinions; all of which corresponds to the systematic torsion of fact between the narrow shores of a reality and a culture subjected to any government.

But even the creature dirtied by the most vile profession is quick to salvage the instant in which he feels the boil of a dark and untranslatable nature: with not even a second thought, he freely perceives, liberated from the symptoms of a reflection of castration and irredeemably bourgeois mental forms. Never, respected Doctor, have you abandoned this repossession of the body that causes the symbols to that which intangibly loses itself at the same moment it is learned to explode and withdraw.

Exiled from such benefits by who knows what demented gene, in the center of a phantasmagorical scene, where now not a muscle or bone is remembered, you have produced the unreal material of a wooden skeleton, the undoing of a fundamental chaffing that had sealed off a being in its primary strengths and explosive capacities where this being let the acts of legal barbarity deposit its excesses in those lagoons, hieroglyphic and never delineated from its body trance and body resurrection.

It has never been a magistrate's job to promote the unlimited connection of a practical situation to the liberating moment of a certain brutal counter language, material, upheld by that which is most hidden, and so disposed to make it appear, while pulverizing style, conventions, syntax and lexicon, all of the lymphatic real repressed by the education of a certain espectorated symbolic. This self creation doesn't consent to being framed by the trigonometry of any practice, it doesn't want to give itself up to counselors or mediators, and, inadmissable, it raises itself up for argument since it isn't about some theory susceptible to being catalogued, integrated in the hum and destined, once more, to frustrate the downward climb by the chain links and capillaries of the spirit. Your trousers of a public functionary don't empower nor grant you carte blanche to the radiographic responsibility of this sexual bottom floor, blind and worsened by codes, that should, before anything, take precautions against a will that has not been able to cease allowing it to suffer the interventions of a science of thought.

Against these illusions, you have not limited yourself to shitting on your institutional creature's plot—while you should avoid, at whatever cost, inserting yourself in your marrow's most secret and burning expectorations—but have invaded, in the manner of some grandiloquent bacteria that can no longer subsist among the detrituses of public institutions, the most intimate dance of this physical language, at once compact and never closed, at once flat and entirely open, that had been reserved at the margen of whatever societal alibi.

You can't do anything about this even if you were to brand the syndicates' corrosive signs, to make a thousand and one decrees upon the Chamber's repressive cellular brushes, to try, infiltrating the christs of their althetic fervor, to win over the masses. But, we can't forgive you now that you, with an idiotic smile, have swallowed the eruption of suffering and this pneumatic flow that shamelessly emmanates from the most oppressed of your internal realms so that your stomach becomes a galstragia, your brain, menengitis, your eye, the lingering gaze of a jeering yogi.

As such, you have progressed in your descent: far from and beyond rising above your misery of a certain official and contingent ritual, you have put yourself in the center of our daily life like a deformed mirror, a badly demented looking glass that hastens to reflect us in an obscene amplification of our organic erosions and stagnant fibers, pretending that, by some luck, a fatal apoplexy, induced to the complete landscape of the juices and nerve endings of thought, separates us at the axis and deposits us without remission in a crystalized stroke.

You can't conceive of this shit except as the agonizing work of a zombie that understands that he can only be loved by a hopeless community, short-tailed ontologicide buried in its own labyrinth and forced to fraternize because of the worms of its eternity.

Beneath this specular and narcististic unity that sheds itself like a shell and hides us and that you commend yourself to methodically nourish with the injection of your facial traumas and your nueralgic mysticisms, we still breath in a certain atomized refuge of being, the hide out of an open systole and a magnetic eroticizacion, latent on account of that whirlpool of commotions which churns over a sensibility that has never been inscribed and on account of those skies of passionate errancy rubbed incessantly at the extreme edges of the spine.

Here, there is still a boldness of penetration and wit that excuses the self-satisfied word and turns it against its own body to the point of perforating it; that continues to create in unavoidable secret brilliant holes and in other worlds; that turns an alley without exit into a drum roll of strength and doubt into the very material of assault; that, with each rotation, traces a foundation and gives it back converted in vomit; and that no longer thinks about multiple modes of existence as a formulated density but as the indecent blood of an abyss whose borders open up.

We haven't lost, esteemed Doctor, this material - scratched up and disorderly because of the traversal of itself - converted into a floor of canals and orifices through which air, urine, sweat, vibrations, mucus, smells, saliva and lymph pass; that allows, thanks to such humours, it to contract and work itself up until altering, and even denaturalizing, the apparatus that socializes and rationalizes it.

We summon, even in our insignificance, this unproposed state of exaltation, transformation and desire, whose emotions don't ask about those to which they are linked neither by that in which they could affix themselves to and to that, by a stroke of phlegmatic revindication of themselves, which lends the nerves those images that bear the very fulgency of things, this knowledge that possesses as much its mass as its lucidity, its entanglements as its dislocations.

Our true life, Mr. President, occurs in those instances in which a certain state of absurdity and abolition takes place with its greatest receptivity; and in which, through the cracks of a reality, inviable from the beginning, a manifestly enigmatic world speaks.

We care about this uninjured world of the mummified skies and the fossilized wakes of the brain, of that false leadership that proposes to construct the spirit with its long-winded speeches about the morals and laws of man, of those horrendous jails of blood that establishes collective meaning among its mineral breaths. We can't, esteemed Doctor, eternally breath the salvos of cadavers that swirl about there where a germinal head has yielded to the cowardly contracts of its own thoughts.

We don't hesitate to let you know that we have woken up today on account of a paroxysmal shaking of the limbs and the evidence that this new body, scanned and rythmic, has brought to light the motorized conditions for an insurrection of all beginnings.

We let you know that this anatomy of volcanos, of tides and winds that surrounds us refuses to go on denouncing the curse of a monacled image and, indisposed to suffer yet again the limits of a physical contraction, doesn't hesitate to declare a war to the death on whatever anthropomorcentric conspiracy.

We let you know that we no longer fear those black masses responsible for propagating your impassible and petulant gravitations, most definitely conjured by a body that recognizes the dynamite whose discharges don't wish to be oriented or sublimated in some sense.

We let you know that any cadaver that aspires to occupy the seat of honor of an inevitable sensation rots, contaminated, in its own waste.

We let you know that for each thousand burning pathogenies dedicated to the unraveling of the deterioratization of a disabled multitude, for each thousand vociferations where the hammers of an usufructary language are wielded, there is a proliferating world of a precocious lunatic and his birth at all levels of life.

We let you know that the gods of this *hallucant* insanity have been multiplied in the sewers of being and an ecstasy superior to the motives of whatever crime overflows the dikes.

We let you know that a force of expectoration strained of all cerebral desclassifications will have no pity for that which has relinguished the bare act to make its own position surface instead.

We let you know that we have beeen born of the clear and impure elements of our circulation and not the decisions of some democratic father and from today on the words of his supreme excellence will constitute the pit of consciousness in which we will throw the excremental material of our rites.

We let you know that each true experience of communion can't be born but of a thought bound to the flesh, a thought that doesn't cease to rise above the crystalized operations of reason and, thanks to that, the concert of things and beings are freed of the limited manners of an assembly of objects.

We let you know that the substratum of man is constructed with a marvellous imperfection of accents, with frayed points that are lost in the perimeters of a brain that thinks with echoes of unpronounceable words, the urgency of lightening bolts in a dense sky, with salvos of error that perforate and illuminate the unknown, with suspended images balanced in the nuetral point between good and bad solicitations, with bottomless errors of the mind where riches are squandered and where spiritual or sensual seasons no longer matter.

We let you know that having escaped the accidents and cataclysms of the flesh has, at the same time, erradicated the marvellous possibility of reflecting upon its illnesses, depriving it of an extreme source of imagination. Instead, you have taken refuge in this hide out of notions where the putrification of life wastes no time in incubating.

We let you know that the crucifying threads that join us to your sclerosis have been cut by a storm of errant sparks and serendipitous phosophorence and that we have stopped this way of retaining the obscene title of the public servants of a point of view, of the ticks of an era and species which abuse reality.

We let you know that your being impotent to cross the border of appearances, and taking care to not cover your tracks, has destroyed the last hope of being reborn in the supreme intellectuality of a physiological sky, and that this limited frame of weakness and functional cowardice only allows you to summon this hybrid procession of bloody inmates and violated things.

We let you know that a nightmare of limbs opens its flight to the summits, that the suffering angles run a course to the confines of intelligence, that the mental stalactites bury the dosage of a mobilizing chill in the poem, that the unsuspected manias of fate only conduct language to the drooling truth, that the dreaming heads bleat in their cocoons, that nonsense causes the nervous rays of lightening to stand on end, that voices without membrane copulate in an anticipated adultery, that the absurd hours ignite sulfatases in the mind, that the impressions of a palpitating beauty dulls visions and make the futures quiver.

We let you know that the sphynx pregnant with worms is about to explode.

Roberto Cignoni
tr. K.A. Kopple

Issue #10

When they asked the presidential candidate which books he liked to read, he answered that he liked to read the works of Socrates. While reading them he perhaps ran across the famous paradox known as "the paradox of the liar," attributed to Epimenides, a Cretian who said, "all Cretians are liars," which at the time perplexed the Greeks. A paradox of the liar exists today, which also perplexes some Argentines. But first of all, the paradox must be translated differently to conserve its meaning. A local approximation might be: The Liar says, "Follow me, I won't defraud you," after which he defrauds them again and then says, "Follow me, I won't defraud you." The utterance is not of course paradoxical but the result is: the Liar defrauds once again and once again the defraudees follow him.

Political deception is not a novelty, neither are liars: there were, there are, and there will be millions. The question is why the hundreds of thousands repeatedly victimized by the Liar continue supporting him. In a famous story, a lying little boy deceived the villagers crying "wolf, wolf!" so they would save him but, after several consecutive lies, when the wolf actually came, no one helped him. Curiously, the villagers of a certain country in America's Southern Cone are fooled each time they respond to the call and continue responding each time they are called. A people that believes in a Liar knowing what he is: it is difficult to imagine a stranger political phenomenon. A congenital defect in the social intellect? An inexplicable phenomenon of collective auto-flagelation? The explanation proposed here is of another order: many people respond each time the Liar demands it knowing they will be defrauded, not because they truly want to be but because they suffer from blackmail and, in this situation, they have no choice. A good number of the voters are trapped in a situation similar to that imposed by the mafia: it threatens them with a future harm, and, in exchange for avoiding it, demands they pay a price, "collaborate." The "bad" with which it threatens them is that, if they do not support the government, the abyss opens up, Argentina falls into hyperinflation, social chaos, hunger and distaster. An extortion of a fearful and hypersensitive people by means of a future terror. Many humble and average homes - in addition to being in debt with loans in foreign money - fear that if the actual policy changes, their families will suffer an irreversible economic harm. They prefer to "collaborate," although they detest the Liar and his political deceptions, rather than run the risk of having the threat carried out.

Even the political opposition falls victim to blackmail. For political reasons, it believes that it is convenient to go on affirming that this is a democracy, maintaining the fiction in defense of continuity, the possibility of a future representative democracy. To shut up or speak up with euphanisms in fear of destabilizing the future democratic system is also to be blackmailed.

A people which follows a politician who they don't want and criticize out of fear. This is the best indication of the political situation in which they are living: a situation typically undemocratic. The constitution says that the government should be a republic and the sine qua non condition of a republic is the division of power. In Argentina, the legislative branch does not legislate but mainly limits itself to voting on the executive branches orders. The judicial branch, with its subordinate supreme court, does not ultimately judge but sentences at the executive branches' indication. In order to win a legislative vote, the goverment party does not hesitate to put a false deputy on the bench. It has even "made" an unfavorable supreme court judgement "disappear" and then replaced it. It fixed various elections - including the one for governor (Santiago del Estero) - twisting the popular will. It intervened in the provinces. It annuled their administrative powers or suppressed them with additional personnel. The press, when it didn't humble itself, suffered from different kinds of political and economic pressure and, if this didn't work, was threatened, even journalists and instalations were physically assaulted. In this political situation, the Liar refers to this state of affairs as a true democracy and adds that the country "never enjoyed such liberty," which are the Liardiagnostician's words to the effect that reality is precisely the opposite. There is in force an autocratic governmental regime under which the executive branch stealthily wants to retain the sum of the political power and under which the democratic institutions are maintained, according to the Liar's policy, as decoration to conceal the function of a government that desires the absolute concentration of power and the absence of oppositions and regulations.

Once the Liar, now in power, affirmed that he will be the governor remembered, before all else, for the innauguration of the National Library and then ordered it to be inaugurated. By decree, and on a certain date, he declared finished a building that was not finished and innaugurated an empty library without books. To top it off, he closed the old National Library, where there were books, so that the readers were without books or their rights as readers. Seventeen months later, the transfer complete, the old building's (approximately) two million volumes were reduced to eight hundred thousand. Did they ruin and lose a million two hundred thousand books? Or were they made to disappear to speed up the transfer? In the 16th century, a muslim caliph had the Library of Alexandria burned with its 300.000 volumes, some of which could be found in no other library and could now never be read. Will this other caliph be remembered for having innaugurated a building which was unfinished and could not function or, for a new monstrous record, having liquidated the equivalent of four Libraries of Alexandria? It is said that the Caliph Omar burned the books in homage to the truth, to his dubious truth according to which these books, whether they corresponded or contradicted the Koran, were useless and should be burned: the homage to the Liar's truth can only be a lie.

These are the cretian methods of the Lying being. Spectral changes, scene changes, disguised apparitions and verbal threats behind which distinct occurences take place. The spectacle is the veil of the spectral, which is apparition without life. They arm themselves with decorations that have nothing to do with reality or, better yet, have something to do with it inasmuch as they veil reality for those who do not stop trying to perceive it.

The affirmation that the state cannot create a culture is partially true and partially false. It cannot write the movement of a symphony or paint a picture or imagine a poem but culture neither begins nor ends with art. Education, for example, creates culture. And the actual government carries out educational functions: it offers a successful model, that of the corrupt, which it does not shamefully hide: it displays it, defends it, gives it elementary responsibilities and, what is even more terrible, guarantees its impunity. This is its pedagogical attitude. Teach the population, above all the youngest, that corruption is socially acceptable: many strive for it, they chose the corrupt life. The harm that produces and reproduces in society the multiplication of the corrupted cannot be healed from one day to another. It leaves a mark which is difficult to erase, which the Liar's presents as his success.

If in truth a writer's homeland is her or his language and that the writer conscientiously collaborates in its construction, she or he has the responsibility to avoid, whatever it may be, yet another scam. General corruption, like governmental policy, embraces this typically cretian act: for example, it assumes that, like the little boy, truth or falsehood are equivalent, that in matters of language anything goes if it serves the Liar's interests. We say at least, in this humble defense of language, that truth and falsehood are not equivalent. Language has its own rules and its own effects that the autocrat can take advantage of but which he does not control. And no autocrat devoted to the lie as linguistic style can cause this exploitation to last infinitely: in the end, it will last as long as the autocrat, a portion of time that if remembered is because of its disastrous effects. No doubt, they shall preceed him in the fall.

tr. K.A. Kopple

List of contributors published by XUL.

#1: Yasao Akeda; Rodolfo Alonso; Ichiro Ando; Alfonso Barrera; Guillermo Boido; Lobo Boquincho; Takuboku Ishikawa; Ozaki Hoya; Reinaldo Jimenez; Otani Joseki; Takeko Kujo; Yone Noguchi; Cesare Pavese; Jorge Santiago Perednik; Victor Redondo; Jorge Ricardo; Guillermo Roig; Yasao Saijo; Leonardo Scolnik; Ogiwara Seinsensui; Xul Solar; Iku Takenaka; Susana Villalba; Akiko Yosano.

#2: Gabriele-Aldo-Bertozzi; Guilermo Boido; Haroldo de Campos; Inés Cook; Alfonso Cisneros Cox; Carlos López Degregori; Rodolfo Fogwill; Laura Klein; Manuel Martínez; Mario Montalbetti; Nicolás Rosa; Pier Paolo Pasolini; Jorge Santiago Perednik; Néstor Perlongher; Beatriz Sarlo; Angel Rivero; Luis Thonis.

#3: Roland Barthes; Arturo Carrera; Javier Cófreces; Emeterio Cerro; Rey Don Denis de Portugal; Yosef el Escriba; Fernando Esquío; Roberto Ferro; Miguel Gaya; Paio Gomez Chariño; Jonio González; Yehuda Ha Levy; Marcias; Susana Poujol; Horacio Quiroga; Angel Rivero; Fernando Rodríguez Izquierdo; Alfonso el Sabio; Don Sancho I; Nahuel Santana; Pero Viviaez

#4: Raúl Gustavo Aguirre; César Aira; Ramón Alcalde; Oswald de Andrade; Alcides Buss; Augusto de Campos; Haroldo de Campos; Arturo Carrera; Susana Cerdá; Mário Chamie; Ferreira Gullar; José Hernández; Francisco Madariaga; Rodolfo Modern; Ricardo Montiel; Héctor Piccoli; Décio Pignatari; Cassiano Ricardo; Nahuel Santana; Cid Seixas; Sousândrade; Raúl Vera Ocampo.

#5: Arturo Carrera; Susana Cerdá; Emeterio Cerro; Martín Chanetón; Susana Chevasco; Roberto Ferro; Jorge Santiago Perednik; Néstor Perlongher; Gustavo Röessler; Nahuel Santana; Luis Thonis; Román Sluszkiewicz.

#6: César Aira; Jorge Luis Borges; Arturo Carrera; Emeterio Cerro; Arturo Cuadrado; A.E.G.; Oliverio Girondo; Roberto Ferro; Francisco Madariaga; Enrique Molina; Olga Orozco; Jorge Santiago Perednik; Néstor Perlongher; Alfredo Rubione; Nahuel Santana; Jorge Schwartz; Luis Thonis.

#7: Sergio Bizzio; Arturo Carrera; Susana Cerdá; Emeterio Cerro; Roberto Cignoni; Marcelo Di Marco; Roberto Ferro; Reinaldo Laddaga; Jorge Lépore; Miguel Loeb; Jorge Santiago Perednik; Néstor Perlongher; Susana Pujol; Sergio Rondán; Gustavo Röessler; Hugo Savino; Nahuel Santana; Luis Thonis.

#8 (in preparation)

#9: Ramón Alcalde; Antonin Artaud; J.J. Bajarlía; Lord Byron; Camoens; Roberto Cignoni; Luis Chitarroni; Florencia Dassen; Gilles Deleuze; Roberto Ferro; Amadeo Gravino; Goethe; Jorge Lépore; Hilda Mans; Higinio Martínez; Graciela Nakagawa; Vladimir Nabokov; Jorge Santiago Perednik; Daniel Rodriguez Mujica; Ricardo Rojas Ayrala; Nahuel Santana; Kuniko Sasaki; Amalia Sato; Shelley; Sei Shonagon; Phillip Sollers; Luis Thonis; Louis Wolfson.

#10: Marcel Bernabau; Ricardo Castro; Roberto Cignoni; Marcel Duchamp; Fabio Doctorovich; Lilian Escobar; Carlos Estévez; Lydia Gal; Raúl García; Raymond Queneau; François Le Lionais; Jean Lescure; Jorge Lépore; Georges Perec; Jorge Santiago Perednik; Juan Pérez; Angel Rivero; Jaques Roubaud; Gustavo Röessler; Ricardo Rojas Ayrala; Roberto Sheines; Edgardo Vigo.

#11: Rodolfo Alvarez; Charles Bernstein; Roberto Cignoni; Jaques Derrida; Andrea Gagliardi; Raúl García; Ariel Gombert; Osvaldo Lamborghini; Ernesto Livon Grosman; Jorge E. Mendez; Milita Molina; Jorge Santiago Perednik; Sergio Rigazio;Ricardo Rojas Ayrala.

134

A Brief Note About the Translators

Jorge Guitart, a Cuban by birth, has published poetry in English in the U.S. and in Spanish in the U.S., Spain, and Latin America. In recent years he has been writing almost exclusively in English. He has recent work published or forthcoming in *Exquisite Corpse, First Intensity, Snail's Pace Review, Linden Lane Magazine, Kiosk, 6ix, Situation*, and *Open 24 Hours*. Since 1973, he has taught at the State University of New York at Buffalo.

Kathryn A. Kopple is a specialist in contemporary Latin American literature. Translations includes *Subchamber* by the Argentine poet Mercedes Roffé, *The March Hare* by the Uruguayan writer Marosa Di Giorgio and "Dark Tears of a Mere Sleeper" by the Mexican writer Ana Clavel. Her translations have appeared in literary reviews and anthologies in Canada and the United States: including Marjorie Agosín's *These Are Not Sweet Girls* (1994), *Exact Change Yearbook* (1995), *Fiction International* 25, *Seneca Review* 1993. In 1993, *Sonora Review* awarded her second prize for her translation of Mercedes Roffé's "Poem #34."

G. J. Racz's translations of Benito Pérez Galdós's historical novel *Gerona* was published by the Edwin Mellen Press. His translations of the poetry of the Andalusian José Manuel del Pino and the Peruvian José Antonio Mazzotti have appeared in several journals. He is currently at work on a bilingual edition of the fables of Felix María Samaniego.

Graciela Sidoli, who especializes in the Italian Avant-Garde, is presently working on a translation of one of Marinetti's collection of short stories. As the literary translator of the Italian poet Paolo Valesio, she has published in various journals in Italy and the US. As the editor of *PolyText,* she has presented yearly translations of the most prominent Italian poets, among them Antonia Porta, Adriano Spatola, Maurizio Cucchi, and others.

Molly Weigel has been translating poets from XUL for more than ten years. Her translations of Susana Cerdá, Jorge Santiago Perednik and Néstor Perlongher, among others, have appeared in *APR, Sulfur, Rift* and *Exact Change Yearbook*. She holds a PhD from Princeton University. She is presently working on a book provisionally titled *Interactive Poetics: Native-American/European-American Encounter as a Model for Poetic Practice* which explores the work of Williams, Olson, Howe and Rothenberg.

ROOF BOOKS
Partial List

Andrews, Bruce. **EX WHY ZEE**. 112p. $10.95.
Andrews, Bruce. **Getting Ready To Have Been Frightened**. 116p. $7.50.
Benson, Steve. **Blue Book**. Copub. with The Figures. 250p. $12.50
Bernstein, Charles. **Islets/Irritations**. 112p. $9.95.
Bernstein, Charles (editor). **The Politics of Poetic Form**. 246p. $12.95; cloth $21.95.
Brossard, Nicole. **Picture Theory**. 188p. $11.95.
Child, Abigail. Scatter Matrix. 79p. $9.95.
Davies, Alan. **Active 24 Hours**. 100p. $5.
Davies, Alan. **Signage**. 184p. $11.
Davies, Alan. **Rave**. 64p. $7.95.
Day, Jean. **A Young Recruit**. 58p. $6.
Di Palma, Ray. **Motion of the Cypher**. 112p. $10.95.
Di Palma, Ray. **Raik**. 100p. $9.95.
Doris, Stacy. **Kildare**. 104p. $9.95.
Dreyer, Lynne. **The White Museum**. 80p. $6.
Edwards, Ken. **Good Science**. 80p. $9.95.
Eigner, Larry. **Areas Lights Heights**. 182p. $12, $22 (cloth).
Gizzi, Michael. **Continental Harmonies**. 92p. $8.95.
Gottlieb, Michael. **Ninety-Six Tears**. 88p. $5.
Grenier, Robert. **A Day at the Beach**. 80p. $6.
Hills, Henry. **Making Money**. 72p. $7.50. VHS videotape $24.95. Book & tape $29.95.
Hunt, Erica. **Local History**. 80 p. $9.95.
Inman, P. **Criss Cross**. 64 p. $7.95.
Inman, P. **Red Shift**. 64p. $6.
Lazer, Hank. **Doublespace**. 192 p. $12.
Mac Low, Jackson. **Representative Works: 1938–1985**. 360p. $12.95, $18.95 (cloth).
Mac Low, Jackson. **Twenties**. 112p. $8.95.
Moriarty, Laura. **Rondeaux**. 107p. $8.
Neilson, Melanie. **Civil Noir**. 96p. $8.95.
Pearson, Ted. **Planetary Gear**. 72p. $8.95.
Perelman, Bob. **Virtual Reality**. 80p. $9.95.
Piombino, Nick, **The Boundary of Blur**. 128p. $13.95.
Raworth, Tom. Clean & Will-Lit. 106p. $10.95.
Robinson, Kit. **Balance Sheet**. 112 p. $9.95.
Robinson, Kit. **Ice Cubes**. 96p. $6.
Scalapino, Leslie. **Objects in the Terrifying Tense Longing from Taking Place**. 88p. $9.95.
Seaton, Peter. **The Son Master**. 64p. $5.
Sherry, James. **Popular Fiction**. 84p. $6.
Silliman, Ron. **The New Sentence**. 200p. $10.
Silliman, Ron. **N/O**. 112 p. $10.95.
Templeton, Fiona. **YOU—The City**. 150p. $11.95.
Ward, Diane. **Human Ceiling**. 80p. $8.95.
Ward, Diane. **Relation**. 64p. $7.50.
Watten, Barrett. **Progress**. 122p. $7.50.
Weiner, Hannah. **We Speak Silent**. 72 p. $9.95.

Discounts (same title): 1 – 4 books—20%; 5 or more—40%. .(Postage 4th Class incl., UPS extra)
For complete list or ordering, send check or money order in U.S. dollars to:
SEGUE FOUNDATION, 303 East 8th Street, New York, NY 10009